All You Can Be

Iain Munro

Michael Terence Publishing

First published in paperback by
Michael Terence Publishing in 2021
www.mtp.agency

ISBN 9781800941199

Cover images
courtesy of Iain Munro

Contents

Introduction

I would like to tell you my story and take you on a journey to BE ALL YOU CAN BE. I will give you background through my early life and up to when life changed aged at 25. I hope this experience and in a sense story will help some people, inspire others and maybe make a few people smile? So on that note let me make a start…

My childhood was very happy I had a great family life. I enjoyed school, latterly did not focus as much as I should have done but I am sure that is true for many people. My early childhood was largely spent in Blackpool and from my limited memory of that time in my life, it was very good indeed. My main memories from that time are Auntie Pam's playgroup, Dad's shocking yellow Datsun and my elder brothers mate Bobby. Bobby had me at four believing his next door neighbour was Roland Rat. As a family we moved down south when Dad got a new job and I soon started first school. As I have said I had a lovely childhood and was very privileged and had many great experiences which I didn't appreciate at the time. Looking back I was very fortunate and could not have asked for any more. First and middle school were happy times and I did show flickers of achieving academically. I hasten to add this never came to fruition and is an area of one of my regrets pre life changing at 25. I began at five/six to start a love for Football. I began playing for the local club and whilst being reasonable technically and having some good spells mixed with some bad I would continue playing until 25. I went through this time having some good moments playing for some good sides but never really pushing myself to get fit change my lifestyle and get to the best I could be. Now I want to be careful here I do not want to paint a picture that I was the next David Beckham as I was never of any particular standard. In the words of Dave Nicholas "Let's be clear you where rubbish at football". That said I maybe could have achieved slightly more as a young adult. That is quite possibly a big maybe. Again let's be very clear. I was not very good but maybe could have done a little better if I had committed. So forming part of one of my three regrets from life pre 25 is my last year at secondary school. I was academically ok but my school reports often read find it hard to fully focus and could do better. My regret here is I was very sociable and found it difficult to turn this off. In my early days I had problems finding my way socially and wanting to be involved with everybody and not really understanding how to fit in with all groups. This meant that at times my behaviour at secondary school was a little erratic and at times a bit Jekyll and Hyde depending on what group I had decided I was part of on that particular day. So it came to exams and although I still wound up with the grades I needed to start my A levels looking back at this period there are regrets as I could have achieved much more. Not for one second am I saying I was Einstein in waiting but I could have put much more effort in. This as they say we will never know but remains a regret as I know I did not commit and fully engage. My elder brother was a very good footballer and Cricketer. In a way he was my idol in my young days. It would have been good if I had followed his lead in certain areas that would have saved a few issues later in life. Now I have given some background let's fast forward to me starting work in August 1997. I decided to opt out of my A levels and went to work with one of my best mates at a Computer reseller. I was transfixed on being a salesman earning bundles of cash driving a Porsche and having the stunner on my arm. I hasten to add this never happened. Although I did OK and for my age earned reasonable money my problems started as I had no appreciation for money and would never live within my means. I did a number of roles within the reseller before I eventually followed my mate (Stuy – a good Mate and Australia team mate) to a new company and got a bit further involved in a sales team. Stuy had introduced me to both companies. Although I was not perfect I would like to think I was polite and got on well with people. I believed at the time this would get me further up the ladder. It didn't and professionally and sportingly my regrets are never fully committing to things and becoming super fit or well versed in the products. This leads me to my other regret at this time. Never pushing myself. Always just doing enough to get by. This is my advice to young people today. Commit to things and push yourself as you will live to regret not putting the effort in. In my younger days I was not rude and like to think perhaps unlike today's generation I did have some respect for people. Many may disagree with this as in my young days I was fairly arrogant and up for a good time. I had some wonderful holidays, nights out football trips and just a great time from 17-25. I was surrounded by great friends and had the ability to get along with my peers and the older generation. I have a great family and I am very lucky with the position I am in. In my younger days I would often drink too much and looking back this may have been a coping mechanism for the sense of not achieving. Although I had a good time the evil of money was always an issue. I would never live within my means and was forever stressed and chasing something never fully understanding what. In my early twenties I went travelling with three of the best (Stuy, Graham and Gus). We had a great time and went to New Zealand then lived in Sydney for six months. I had no choice then but to live within my means but life was easier then as it was just a party. New Zealand has another smaller regret in life. All I will say is arrogance played a part and the regret is "THE PRETTY CANADIAN"!

I came home and went back to the company I had left 10 months earlier. From here I did not want to live at home any longer so I became the lodger at a Friends house in the centre of town. I had a great time for a number of years and really did not grow up financially. I continued life as one big party whether I could afford it or not. I made some good friends at this time in my life and they remain good friends today. The drinking culture was rife. I would often drink most days in a week and would subsequently call in sick to my job. In the group I was in the weeks drinking was named the following. Monday Mayhem – Tornado Tuesday – Wa HEY Wednesday – Thunderball Thursday – Free for all Friday – SATURDAY (after football) – SUPER SUNDAY (after football). I had moved company and was surrounded by good people and I could have set myself up. Regrets I have a few. One being I went to work for the best people and although I had good experiences with them should of could of would of made more of this time. At this time I worked directly for Trav and the company owner Neil Ledger. They were both great to me along with my direct boss Parkie. I could maybe have done more here but they were very good to me and Mr Ledger in particular went above and beyond after things changed. In the heavy drinking party days I would often go out most nights and all day on a Sunday. By 25 I was at a cross roads. I had just split from a girlfriend which was in no way a catalyst but I was starting to come off the rails slightly. I had stayed on a party always drinking too much (Because I am also a rubbish drinker!) and would sometimes get myself involved in things I should not. This is a huge regret. This went on for about a nine-month period on and off. I was so low and insecure I always wanted to push things. I am sure my mates would look at me and think why? It was masking my insecurities. I was about to change jobs and had big plans to settle everything down. We will never know if I could have got my head down and settled. Then things changed and in one moment life changed forever.

28th August 2006 20.43

This was the time everything changed. Life would never be the same and I would enter into a battle I could never have comprehended previously. I went to my local pub to watch a Monday night football match. I forget who the game was. For the first time ever I decided to leave at half time and judging by the time just before. I decided I would go as I was in the last week working for the diamond that is Neil Ledger. It will become apparent later why I hold him in such high regards. I left the pub after a few beers and while what follows could be deemed a consequence to this it actually saved my life according to medical experts. I left the pub and stood at the edge of a particularly busy road opposite to where I lived. This is where it all starts to get a bit blurry. I recall the road being very busy and the single carriage road was bumper to bumper on the first carriageway which was moving from left to right. I decided to cross halfway as it was that busy. I moved quickly to the middle and then life changed. The road is on a slight bend and I was hit at between 40-42Mph in the middle of the road. It is not necessary to expand any further on this as I am not bitter and it does not factually alter the following years. A ford focus hit me at between 40-42Mph and after rolling up the bonnet and windscreen was catapulted as high as the pub. This is a two-storey building. My friends saw the impact from inside and more disturbingly for those witnesses heard it. I am told by witnesses sometime later that I was sent as high as the pub spinning like a top. Then comes the painful part. At least I would confirm this if I had any recollection. I hit the carriageway and the noise allegedly was an egg cracking. I am then told I had blood bleeding from both ears and the journey had begun. An ex-military man who I was friendly with and would often have a pint with rarely from began the medical treatment. Making sure I was in the correct recovery position etc. The police and paramedics were onsite quick enough and I am told inconvenienced many people as the road network ground to a halt locally. Yet more examples of me being selfish and not thinking of others.

My skull had been shattered on the right hand side of my head. The swelling and subsequent bleeds had started. The bleeds are much like a stroke I guess and the impact will be further explained later. I am now not sure on time periods but the paramedics and police swung into action. The driver was spoken to by the police but as I stated earlier no further details will be discussed as this is not fair on all involved. The paramedics took me to St Peters hospital where I was assessed. At this point the prognosis was not looking favourable as I am told. This may be the time to quote some medical notes but at this time I do not have access. In St Peters hospital I was on a stretcher and as you can imagine not looking in the best of shape. At this point a good friend of mine walked past as he is a paramedic and saw it was me. He said to his colleagues "what is going on?" It was explained that I was being taken to St George's Hospital, Tooting. My mate then asked a doctor "what are we doing here?" The reply was "Taking that to the morgue mate". This is quoted to me at a much later period and my friend took the job off a colleague as in his words "It was the last thing I could ever do for me". I went to St George's and luckily they did not throw the towel in. I was operated on by obviously a very talented surgeon who administered a craniotomy. A craniotomy is having roughly half the skull removed. This allowed room for the fluid to expand and take the pressure off my brain. My family had now been informed and were arriving at St George's. This was when things looked dire as they were urged to sit with me as it did not look favourable I would make it through the night. Thankfully I did and I remained in a coma for a number of weeks. I was obviously not happy with the challenges ahead so we threw MRSA and meningitis in for good measure. I subconsciously rolled my sleeves up and got on with it. Not really a characteristic I had displayed previously. I say this as I did not commit to anything apart from drinking having a good time and in very rare moments in sport. I did not really offer any resistance to a negative situation. This was also a tricky time as I had been on a party for months with little regard for myself so I believe general health and body well-being was not perfect. I believe this was an awkward conversation for my brother too have with my Dad, because neither thought I would be so stupid and reckless. This is something that is regrettable and although not an alcoholic or dangerously over the top I was young and a bit carefree and careless, in hindsight my lifestyle could have been a lot better.

Paragraph from St George's Hospital

"Iain was admitted in the early hours of August 29, 2006. He had been hit by a car and was in coma from a life-threatening head injury. He had an emergency operation to remove a blood clot from around his brain, and part of his skull on the right side was removed to give his brain room to swell. After a fairly stormy initial recovery in the Intensive Care Unit, he then made really rapid progress and was transferred back to his local hospital - St Peter's - at the end of September, followed by a period of rehabilitation at the Bradley Unit. Iain had further surgery in July 2007 to reconstruct his skull with a titanium plate and has gone on to make a really remarkable recovery overall."

Who am I to correct but some of the above dates in my mind are not 100% accurate. Please refer to the dates I have given and if I am slightly incorrect please remember I have had a serious head injury!

The image on the front cover shows the staples holding the skin of my scalp together. This is where the surgeons entered to remove the right hand side of my skull. Below are brain scans which show quite a bleed. The third image is a normal brain scan taken from Google images. The top two images are my brain scans which show some swelling and bleeds.

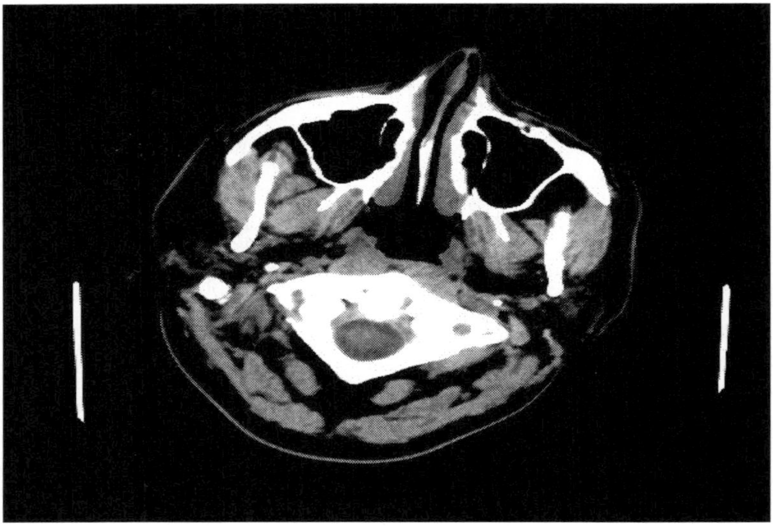

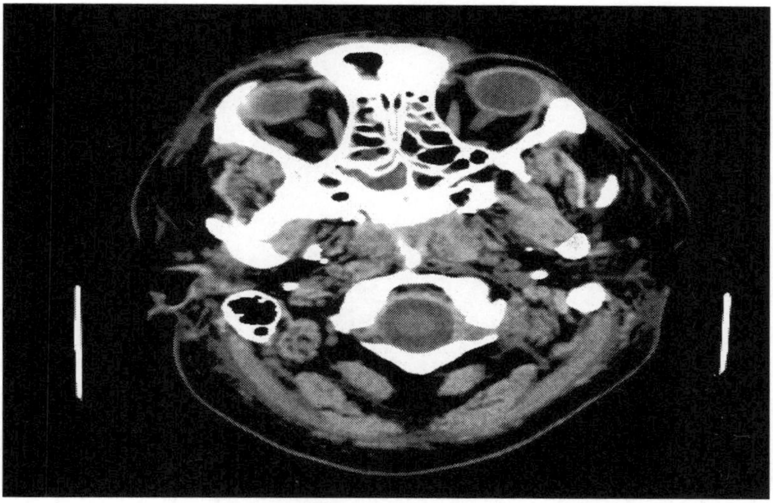

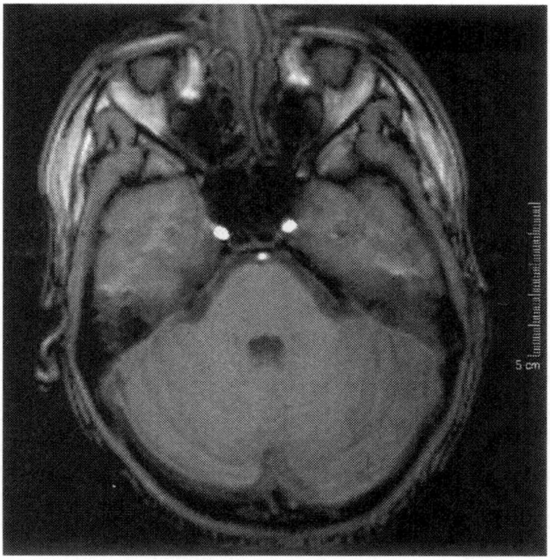
5 cm

Recovery Begins

Now the recovery is underway if I could of I would have liked to thank everyone individually for getting me to this point. All of the medical staff the Police my mates at the Pub who did what they could to give me a shot, especially the military man. My Friend the paramedic as we will call him for now. I have other descriptive words that would work but not for this time. Now we are underway on the road to recovery. The early days of recovery I have to go on eye witness accounts from people close to me as I have zero memory of this time. Admittedly I spent an amount of this time in a coma, but when I was out I have no recollection of discussions scenarios or visits. I was lucky I received a number of visits from a lot of people. I am told a number of people found this very difficult. This suggests to me that although in my eyes I was arrogant at times and a bit obnoxious. Never committing to anything and just on a bit of a party I was not a complete TWAT! That said in the future I wanted to change the way I was perceived by people and how I went about my life. At this point I can once again only say thank you for the support I received at this time. I hope this helped my family a bit and although I was not in a position to appreciate it consciously I am sure on one level this aided them through this tough period. When I first woke from the coma I found communication almost non-existent and needed help to hold my own head. If I was moved from my bed I am told this required a hoist. At this time I have no recollection of these problems. From here I began to get stronger and in time (a short period). I began to speak and attempt to walk. There was a time of not always staying upright and the slightest smallest distance looking like Bambi on Ice. I think at this time I was in the best place as I have no recollection of this time but it must have been very difficult for my friends and family to get used to.

Whilst in St George's on the Atkinson Morley wing my elder brother (Neil) came to visit me after football on a Saturday evening. I told him very definitely that Brad Pitt and George Clooney had been in to visit me. This caused a lot of confusion as they clearly had not. This was signs that my brain was starting to repair itself as after some investigation it transpired that they had been on TV earlier that day. I believe at that time they may have been promoting an Oceans 11 film but once again I could be wrong. If I am I will use my standard excuse for everything "Serious Brain Injury". So after seeing them both on TV my brain decided they were talking to me and I was convinced that they were in the ward. This was after a previous Visit I had told Neil that Sheffield United had won the World Cup. Yet another indication that I could put some scenarios together that were sort of in the correct field. In this case Sheffield United played football. Unfortunately away from that the brain was talking gibberish and could not even put fabrications or confusion into the correct context. I had a steady flow of visitors and I made gradual improvements as the days went on. These improvements seemed quite vast because of the level I started at. I was transferred to St Peters which is closer to home after a couple of weeks and we are now four to six weeks since the bang on the head. This is what I decided to call the accident. I think this was me subconsciously trying to stay positive and make others feel more comfortable around me. In St Peters my mobility improved vastly and I began to communicate much better. I am told that for large parts of a day I would make perfect sense but then things would become none factual and to use a better term Gibberish. One of my good mates Clarky would come in and I became focussed on we needed to go for a pint. He would try and explain that this was not possible at this time. I would not have it and would begin to invent a scenario to get him to agree with me. In his words "You would jump out of bed. You had this gown on Arse and bollocks hanging out. Put on your trainers and say the nurse has said we can Nip down the crown and grab a beer". He would humour me and explain you can't go you are not dressed for it and you have half your head missing. Nobody would ever say it but at this time I was not looking my best and was looking more like an extra from Hellraiser. My improvement continued but as I have said at this time I have no memory of any of these events. It was approaching the end of October 2006. We are now approaching 8 weeks since the bang on the head. At this time It was discussed that I was making good enough progress to be discharged to a rehabilitation unit that specialised in brain injury rehab.

I do not have the inside track on how the decision was made but I would go to the Ted Bradley Unit to rehabilitate. This is about 1 mile as the crow flies from where I lived. As I got better and arguably got a sense of humour back. Some would argue that I never had one and many would argue I never had one return. I decided to name the unit the Bradley Walsh unit and this is to be what it was known as for many months. Most people would call the unit this but there is a rumour that some people did not realise that this was a tongue in cheek name and I would tell anybody that would listen the unit was called the Bradley Walsh. I think any mistake may have come as I was so convincing that this is what is called. Now we get to the first day I entered the Bradley Walsh. This is the first day I actually remember since the bang on the head. I arrived I believe last day of October 2006 and sat on a sunny day in the small garden area waiting for my room to be ready. This is the first time I remember taking any notice of people I hadn't already met. The person that did this was the receptionist at the Unit. Her Name was Janice and she was a larger than life character and very funny. Speaking with Janice was the first time I felt a bit of normality whatever that was. The best way I think I could describe Janice is Rusty Lee. Just Nice, Loud and mad as a box of frogs. I may have come to this conclusion as visually although they were not identical I believe some people may see my point. That said Janice was much prettier! I remember making that comparison on the day which was a strange one as I was having trouble remembering and recalling things I knew a lot about and people I had known for some time. This being the case the wonder of the brain raises its head as why would I draw the comparison with Rusty Lee. So now I was checked in the rehab could begin. I remember being very tired at this point with the slightest exsurgence of energy wiping me out. Now although I could remember the first day my memory is a bit sketchy to almost non-existent for my first 6 weeks in the unit. I think this is the time when a lot of my mobility and speech and language work was done. I do not recall my level of communication on day one but I am sure it was fairly basic and at times inconsistent. Through these six weeks I am told I worked fairly hard and was rewarded for this by being allowed out of the unit to stay at my Mum's. She took me to watch the side I played for before the bang on the head and see the boys who had been part of the group which provided such support through this time. In one particular game I was in a wheelchair and the pitch was muddy. As part of the warm up they ran over to Mum's car and carried the wheelchair across the field so I was pitchside as the wheels where getting stuck in the muddy surface. I made some steady progress from here and the speech and language therapy and basics like handwriting started again. This did not come easily but it would turn out I am quite a stubborn little fucker and would not let the frustrations beat me. I continued working at things and over time, Quite a short period respectively things improved.

The staff at the Bradley Walsh were magnificent and they worked diligently under quite difficult circumstances. A lot of the patients in the Bradley were recovering from strokes so I was by far and away the youngest in the ward for the first few months. I had always been quite sociable some may say gobby. I found it difficult to strike up any particular bond with any of the other patients or as I started referring to us after a few months to my friends inmates. This is where the staff was so good. I liked a chat and they seemed always happy to do this. If they weren't they hid it very well or maybe not so well as I still was not firing on all cylinders. My initial work in the Bradley Walsh is a bit cloudy as although I remember lots of it the finer details are not at the forefront of my mind. I remember feeling frustrated at many points due to me having a memory that some things I was being asked to do seemed so easy and I could no longer do them on command. This was largely physical but more frustratingly mental and cognitive skills. Getting up in the morning and having a shower took lots of my time and effort. I had to fight the devil in my head saying "sort yourself out. You don't need the seat in the shower or any assistance". The truth of the matter looking back is I probably did but would not allow it. This stubbornness and desire to get better and strong feeling that I wanted to get back to normal spurred me on. I guess this is another message to young people and whoever else wants to listen. If something is worth getting to it often is hard to achieve. If you give up at the first hurdle or things don't go your way you will go through life never achieving any of your goals. I had so much desire to get this right I just kept going at it. Making mistakes and in my mind juvenile issues but going back the next day and just getting on with it until it became second nature and normal. There will hopefully be a number of examples of this as I continue and if somebody can say to themselves "grow up just get on with it, I will try this again another way!" from this message it has been worth putting it on paper.

So in the Bradley Walsh life was starting to seem more normal. A lot of the work in the early days was done by Doctor Song who for some reason I believed looked a lot like my Step Mum Debbie. If I am way off the mark here I will play my serious brain injury card. I use this a lot. In the early days a lot of the work done was very basic things and included learning to look after myself for example showering in the morning and getting up for breakfast. This sounds very simple but it was not as easy as you think trying to get back into a routine. I was incapable of this and subconsciously I become reliant on others to do everything for me. This is were one of the most valuable tools I learnt came into play. I started structuring my day by knowing I needed to be up showered and eaten breakfast by 09.25 to watch Jeremy Kyle. How cool am I? It then became even trendier by me structuring my afternoon around Deal or No Deal. Please don't quote me on this but I believe that was about 16.00. If I am inaccurate I blame my serious brain injury!

This is where things are a bit blurry the early days of the Bradley Walsh. I do not recall a number of the sessions, These being the early speech and language and early physio, OT sessions.

Back to what I can remember. I really start remembering the world and the day to day running order of events about mid-December 2006. It was just past my 26th birthday and I remember thinking I was getting very old. I had a day or two of feeling quite down about this. I remember starting to think this is ridiculous. This is when I came up with the moto I live by now as far as getting older goes. In my situation the reality is that I should not have been here at 25. This being the case anything is a bonus. I try not to forget this and apart from some instances that I will discuss later I try to stay positive. At the end of the day I decided I am lucky to be here. Although the hand I have been dealt is not perfect things are pretty good. I can do more than I ever thought I would be able to. Some of the things I have seen and difficulties others have I am very lucky. This being the case there is always someone worse off than you. Age doesn't bother me now as I am lucky to be able to do what I do and most importantly still be breathing. When you look at things like this you start to sober up on the woe is me talk. So in mid-December I had started getting more freedom which I do not really recall but I am told by Mum that I had been taken out of the unit a number of times. I had been out for dinner and been into Woking shopping. I say shopping wondering about a bit and going to my mate Freds Coffee shop for some Pasta and a cup of Tea. Fred often reminds me he still owes my Dad a fiver for a football bet they had. I certainly cannot remember what it was? Mum had taken me to football a few times in a chair this again I do not really recall. The time before Mid December others will need to fill in whilst I have some memory I do not recall everything and could, for this reason, be inaccurate. So come mid-December I had settled into the unit and after moving rooms a few times was well into the swing of things. I had started to experience some empathy for the first time and understanding others troubles and maybe getting some kindness and selflessness back. One thing about this journey is you become very selfish and the fight for number 1 and your best interests at the time is all you focus on. As I have eluded too the unit was largely made up of elder people as it was a neurological rehab unit a lot of the patients had suffered strokes and such like. This worked for me as I began learning some social skills by interacting without being judged or them having a previous viewpoint on how I was before the bang on the head. I began understanding the rehab and really taking notice as it felt like I was now in a position to work towards a release date. It makes it sound like I was in prison and it really was not like that. In December I regained another emotion that had so far been missing. I started to appreciate the opposite sex again. This was good and at a later date a friend of mine told me an interesting story. I believe these are things that help me mentally come back to nearer how I was previously. He told me that when I had come around and was talking nonsense all of which I can not recall, He was chatting to me and he told me "You do know before the accident you were Gay". Not an issue either way but this was definitely not the case. In my younger days I used to like to think I was a ladies man. The truth of the matter was that is what I always hoped to be I just wasn't very good at it, never in good enough shape, Rich or good looking enough to do so. Anyway I digress. Back to my original point. There was a very pretty physio and I forget her name but this is the first time I had taken notice of any female and thought isn't she nice. I could be crude here but I feel the average bloke knows exactly what I was thinking. She was very nice and always happy to chat and this was the first time I had any interaction other than speaking about my recovery. Now please don't get me wrong the pretty physio would always discuss my recovery but I would then try and initiate a conversation and in fairness to her she would always give me a bit of her time. I can only imagine she was thinking now please shut up but in fairness she did not make her excuses straight away. Like a peacock this got me feeling more self-confident and puffing my chest out a bit. This was the start of me feeling back to normal and it gave me something else to talk about to my friends. Talking to my friends was very helpful although I feel it wasn't great for them at times. My Mum had returned my mobile phone and it was not unheard of to call Gav at 2am on a Wednesday when he had work that morning and ask, "Do you fancy going down the crown for a pint"? I think after about the third or fourth time he stopped explaining that this couldn't happen for the obvious reasons and just plumped for "I Can't Make It"! At this time I must thank my mum for paying my phone bills as they would be upwards of £150 a month when I was in the Bradley Walsh. This was very helpful in my rehabilitation as I would scroll through my contacts of which there were a few and start piecing together how I knew people. This helped the brain kick in and I started to work out a number of friendships and acquaintances. In this time I wished to contact a lot of people that I may not have spoken too for some time but in my mind they had made an impact on me. This must have been weird for some annoying for others but at the time everybody was very generous with their time whether it be a chat or a text message. I wanted to return to NORMAL, Whatever that is as quickly as possible. My memory issues were more short term so if I had known someone for many years I knew them, it did not take me long to fully piece together the jigsaw. The short term memory was very hit and miss but as the days and weeks went on I started wanting to return to normal as much as possible. This is were calling Gav and asking if we can meet for a pint went. This would be a fairly regular occurrence in a standard week. This is one example that sticks in my mind as I have discussed it at a later date and we have had a laugh about it. I was also very keen to try and act as if nothing had happened and plan to do things that in reality I would never be able to achieve or facilitate. Whether that be nights out or dating etc. I think this is where the goal setting allowed me to achieve moving forwards. I always had goals in my mind that I wanted to achieve. Some of which I have achieved many years later some I am still to achieve. I quickly realised that if you constantly set yourself goals that you cannot achieve quickly it becomes very disheartening and frustrating. This is not good for people's mental health as you constantly feel a failure and disillusioned as to how you will achieve your goals. I cannot recall if this was realised in my Phycology sessions with the incredible Drew and latterly Miriam but I realised that setting shorter term more achievable goals is better for you mentally. I will talk further about Phycology a little later. Back to short term goals. My initial goals were simple. Walk with more purpose and straighter and better aligned. In the early days I would be very hunched and frail and not steady at all. This took time and arguably I am still improving but I could measure short term improvements which gave me a huge lift mentally. I would try and remember things daily without writing them down or being prompted. It sounds ever so simple but I guess this is the point of having short term goals. However small or simple in your mind you believe it is you can only be measured from your starting point. This is when I decided it is counterproductive to feel sorry for yourself and measure against others. This is an idealistic behaviour as later you will appreciate this was not always the case and still to this day it is not. I have moments were I think if that had not happened I could be doing this or that. In reality arguably human nature is that you always blame something if you are not where you want to be. The truth of the matter is you cannot look back and think what if. You must make the best of your life not blame circumstance or a chain of events and work positively to achieve short term goals initially. Whilst you are achieving the short term goals which are within your reach with a bit of hard work it is always worth having some longer term goals. These can be a long way off and it is plausible you may not ever get there or it will take some time to do so. It is always worth seeing if these goals can be in some way linked so you can see a progression. This is not a blueprint it is just some ideas. A lot of my longer term goals were physical achievement and at the time of thinking of them seemed a mile away. If you don't have your ultimate goal high you will never push yourself. It is important not to pin all your hopes on being successful in the big dream as the progression you make along the way will be reward enough and make you feel a million times better than you did before you made the small steps towards success. I think the easiest way for me to explain this at this time is to put you in a school scenario. If you are a student who is an E in old money. In your mind the long term goal and the dream would be getting to an A. This will not always be possible but engage and focus and in the process the goals which are achievable will help you structure your way towards the ultimate ending. If the end for you proves to be a C as this is what you can achieve you will feel amazing. This also leaves you room to strive towards the A in the future and keep working hard.

As I have mentioned the first short term goal for me was to walk straighter more upright and completely unaided. This came easy to me and didn't feel like hard work. In my mind I wanted to run and play football again. These were the long term targets and I did not become transfixed on these but always had them in the back of my mind as a target. From the outside I feel many people felt this would never be possible but supported throughout I was. If I am getting my motivation hat on I guess if someone sets out a goal never say It is not possible. Be realistic about the possible problems ahead as my family would often say we will see whenever the subject of me playing football came up. Please bear in mind at this time I had half a skull the fear of anybody knocking me off balance was a worry for everybody and there had not been any talk of the skull reconstruction or as I choose to call it the tin hat. That was given to me at a much later date by a friend of mine. So the journey was now fully under away. Jim the OT (Occupational therapist) challenged me to dibble in and out of cones set quite wide apart in the small rehab gym. This was a very small area so we are talking 4-5 cones. A bit of the old arrogance reappeared as I looked at him flippantly and snarled "are you having a laugh, I can do that with my eyes closed". His reply stuck with me "Go on Then!" I tried to do it and resembled a toddler learning to do this for the first time. I found this extra difficult as one of my main physical problems was the lack of movement strength etc in my left hand side. This was due to the bleeds on the right hand side of my brain. For many weeks post-accident these limbs were non-responsive hence wheelchairs etc. It was the main reason my walking was so troubled and I am probably being a little flippant by giving this a short mention. This effected both my left leg and my left arm and hand. This is the area I still have slight weakness at today. For example I struggle to carry cups or a pint in my left hand without spilling what is inside. Painful with Tea heart-breaking with a Pint! Anyhow back to the dibbling of the football. My initial attempts were pitiful but in fairness to Jim he allowed me to keep at it and we stayed until I could do it to a non Toddler level. I even tried to use my left foot which was unheard of previously! I guess the message here is do not give up if things do not come easily. Put a bit of work into it and show some heart!

This was the start of me wanting to push myself physically. I was made aware that it was good to have goals but not to try and push myself too far. This is the time I had started a Newspaper Club at the beginning of each weekday in rehabilitation. This was good for the mind as you were asked to read sections and as a group be able to identify and discuss certain stories. This was hugely helpful as although the other patients were a lot older and some through the condition were not very sociable or in one instance very friendly, It did help the social aspect of my recovery and for the first time be forced into thinking and trying to process some instruction. I enjoyed this and over the weeks I like to think there was some progress in my ability to read and retain information and discuss with others. For the first time it also got me interested in the outside world. The only thing up until this point that I really focussed on was the football both following professionally and my former team mates. I also wanted to feel like I was still involved socially so whenever I could, I would discuss what was going on with my mates. This helped me formulate in my mind the characters and helped me remember people and put behaviour traits and characteristics to people. It wasn't a case of having a blank canvas but there were lots of grey areas and in some cases just complete black holes. Talking about people and maybe recalling old stories helped to trigger something in the mind which filled in some of these blanks. Anyway I digress back to newspaper club. After a few weeks I was given the responsibility of walking to the local shop and buying the papers for the group. This was good as I had not been outside the unit at this point on my own. I remember the first time I did this I was excited about going out but once out felt very nervous. I walked down the road and passed Woking Police station. This was nervy the first time and then came the one and only time I have had a wobble and a bit of a pull yourself together moment, I had to cross a road. I felt anxious and I must have looked right and left 100 times on a road that was not actually that busy. I eventually crossed the road after having a bit of a chat with myself. I decided; is that how I want to live out my life? Scared or do I just be safe and careful? I eventually talked myself around and got on with it. At times things seem daunting. Don't put yourself in any danger but at times just get on with it! So I got to the shops next to Blockbuster Video and bought the papers. The reason I mention Blockbuster Video is this was a place I often visited with a friend of mine who many question his commitment to life. I don't think anybody really believes this but at that time of his life he was a professional work avoider, as was I on occasions and did not care about much. The King is a very amusing man and good company but we spent hours wasting time at his place with Films a Pizza the King and a four-pack of John Smith's and a packet of fags. This is another example of changing life around. He is now a responsible family man and runs his own business. I use the term responsible loosely! A story of the king. He agreed to help the first team of the club I played for. It was five minutes until the meet time. The then manager asked me to call him and chase him up. The king had been very good and had played a number of leagues higher. When I called to chase him I was met with the following response. "What time is the meet?" I replied "13.30" at 13.25. His reply was "I suppose I better leave then and remember Iain who is doing who the favour here".

Back to the tale so I returned to the Bradley Walsh with the papers and remember feeling pretty good about things and a sense of achievement for the first time in many months. I go back to what I have mentioned previously, Going to the shops and buying newspapers is not a great achievement. But when measured against the starting point it shows a marked improvement. Everybody can have a starting point and the small improvements will have a positive effect and improve motivation to achieve more and confidence to keep striving for more. This limited freedom for a short period of time made me more determined to make as much progress as I could. The fact that I was trusted over all the other inmates also helped my mental health and positive mood. When somebody is working towards bigger goals can they be rewarded throughout the process to help their motivation to achieve? I think it is misconstrued in this day and age that small rewards throughout a process will not mean a huge amount to the person on the journey. It does not have to be of huge monetary value or extravagant but the little things can motivate just as much. Now I had a taste for freedom and could see some light at the end of the tunnel. I wanted more. My memory becomes a lot better now and my Mum gave a list of trusted Adults to the centre so they could take me out for a curry or such like. Just to confirm at this point I was not drinking. Not that this is particularly important in the grand scheme of things. I say this as it times it is important to have a realisation on the situation you are in. As determined as I was to get better and as back to normal as I could (Back to how things were previously), You cannot be irresponsible. I say this as I was still walking around with half a Skull and my movement was still not A1. This meant I was very vulnerable. In fairness to the list they are great fellas but all had the capability in their younger days to be loose cannons. They were great to me. There was No chance of doing anything I shouldn't be doing. This put a bit of fun and helped me structure my week again. It gave me more things to look forward to. I had been having weekends at home with my family which was great and made recovery feel that step closer but adding this additional weekly outing really improved my mental state of mind. It advanced my thinking. It stopped me being too self-obsessed. Whilst it is important to be focussed and driven when you start a journey it is important to have an understanding of others around you. I had lost any empathy for others. It had been all about me. It took many years to work on this and as I will discuss later I was still not there a few years ago and can still have my moments. Today I think I am much better and have moved a further step on from where I was later in the tale. You must never fall into the trap that I am fixed and sorted. If you stop doing the correct things anxiety and self-esteem can become an issue at any time. It is important to keep speaking to people and not become a closed book with the weight of the world on your shoulders. Mental health is important.

So in the unit I was out on a daily basis getting the papers and allowed to leave the unit at weekends (with Family) and on odd occasions with the listed people. This made me more determined to improve and get better. I started to develop a bit more confidence and I was being a lot nicer and more considerate. I do not want to paint a picture that I was an absolute ass before the bang on the head. That said I was a bit selfish however I think fundamentally I was always kind to a point. In my recovery I was eager to remain as focussed as possible and try and be kind. I like to think people would say something along the lines of – a good lad heart in the right place. At times semi amusing and up for a good time but has mellowed and is just a bit nicer than in his younger days. So the journey was well and truly underway. I was always thinking of ways to try and expand my vocabulary, My subjects of conversation and my understanding of the world around me and further a field. This did not happen instantly so I guess the message is don't expect everything to fall into place straight away. When I think that only months before I was being helped out of bed by a hoist and dribbling, To dribble (on command) in and out of cones (However badly) Go for a curry with my mates. Understand and at times participate in a conversation or maybe a bit of banter was a huge level of progress. I did not see this at the time and always wanted more and would strive for the next level. If things are worth getting too and hard to get there it is always worth it in the long run. I didn't really understand at that point where I wanted the journey to finish so I just kept trying and kept pushing myself. At the time it had no effect but as I will discuss later there is a point where you can push yourself too much and lose sight of what you have and always crave more. This can lead to poor mental health. Looking back I should have celebrated what I had done and where I was more when going through the process and not ever thought what if or I should be here. This would have meant depression and self-doubt would not have become an issue. I will discuss this later but at this moment in time it is no longer something I need to fear. I say this as long as I do the correct things. Complacency will let the evil of anxiety take over. As I have heard Tony Adams say before in his battles which are far tougher battles (Addiction) than I have ever fought. "I have the tools". I will discuss this further later. So at this point life was progressing well but I was not happy to let things lie. I wanted the next level of progression. I wanted to run! This sounds something of nothing but my balance was still not A1 and at times it still is not. For example I was advised never to ride a bike again and to this day I have not. This is down to the fact my balance is not good. Especially if I get tired I could well take a tumble. Anyhow away from the self-pity. I wanted to run and I had done and continued to do a bit of work on the exercise bike in the community hospital gym. This made me realise the brief time I had on the bike how unfit I was and spurred me on to do more work. Didn't do much running but did a bit of work with Jim in Woking Park. I was determined but it took time. I was told that for the first few months of running I looked a bit like Bambi on ice. This didn't put me off I just thought I will get better at it! So life continued in the unit and I hope I continued to make improvement. I was beginning to see the fine motor skill benefits of the art class I enrolled in. Every Wednesday Afternoon as a unit those who wanted too would go to the Church over the road and would do the art group run by some local elder parishioners. They were very nice ladies and as well as working on my fine motor skills helped me hugely socially. I had always been quite chatty previously but it was nice to re-focus how to act and communicate with different people. This is another example of changing what I would do normally or pre accident to help me get closer to the end goal. It also got us out of the unit for the afternoon and a bit of cake!

I have spoken about my recovery and this is my perception and my progress may not have been at the levels I felt but the inner feeling of achievement spurred me on to do more. Now we were well into January / February 2007. I was now 26 and the next stage of the recovery was being discussed. The Tin Hat or in normal language the Titanium flap replacement for the 50% of my skull that had been removed. This discussion was exciting at the time and made me feel that things were moving in the right direction!

So discharge day seemed closer and closer. It had now been discussed and I had appointments booked at St George's hospital to discuss the tin hat and this made everything feel like it was moving in the correct direction. I continued to work hard and I was happy to increase what I was doing and the level of effort I needed to put in. I continued to work in the unit and things were getting better and better. I was now allowed out more and more when people were available and life felt like it could return to normal. Whatever normal is? So the procedure had been explained to me and the date was being discussed as early May. We are now in spring and my upcoming release or, in correct terms, discharge was very close. The OT teams had looked at my flat and I had an interesting few sessions with Jim which required me to do some household chores to see I could survive on my own. I never cooked at home so when I made Jim and I a chilli it amazed me that it was edible. I was pretty much ready for the off. I spent a couple of weekends at my flat with my brother acting as minder. I imagine I was never sparkling company for a twenty-four hour period but my brother went above and beyond and even appeared interested. This was a realisation that things had changed and although I may have initially been tempted I realised that at this point I was still very vulnerable so I wanted to take things easy. Physically I was also fairly weak. On discharge from the unit I was measured and weighed. I was told I was 6'1" or thereabouts. I said "I am not I have always been 5'11" ish. It was explained to me that where I had spent lots of time in bed I had not compressed my spine. I guess my message there to anybody who is not the tallest spend six months in bed. I was weighed and the last weight I have in my mind pre bang on the head was 13 stone 5. I was now 8 stone 7. Not looking my best and I am fairly sure half a skull does not equate to that sort of weight loss. So after many months of rehab and sitting in bed touching my individual fingers to the thumb on my left hand to increase mobility. I did this every night and most evenings. I would also Hop from one foot to the other as If I was changing direction to try and improve my balance. Unfortunately I have no photos of me at this time but from what I have been told and what I remember please allow me to paint a picture. I was at that point 6"1 and 8 stone I was skin and bone. I could see my ribs for the first time since a small child. All muscle had wasted (there was very little in the first place). If you can imagine my head at about the centre appeared to dip at a right angle where the skull had been removed. One side skull the right side brain a bit of fluid around the brain and hair had started to grow back. I had veneers put on my teeth shortly before the bang on the head. They where all knocked off in the accident so I had little stubs for front teeth. This part of my journey was coming to an end and the next chapter was about to begin. I have to say a huge thank you to Neil Ledger at this point. He did not need to do this and as I was leaving there was even less reason to do it. He continued to do more than he should for a number of months for my time in hospital I suspect with people in HR or partners questioning why.

I was also now in contact with the late Max Clifford. He had watched my former team play a charity match at Christmas 2006 to raise money for the unit I was in. I kicked the game off with my brother but then left the pitch as I was nowhere near in a position to play any part. Mr Clifford watched the game as he had associates close to the club. He wanted to do something for me personally so we exchanged contact details. We arranged a charity evening which I will discuss later. I can only take as I find and he was a nice man and what would come out later I obviously knew nothing of, or any future allegations so I will refrain from comment. So the discharge day rocketed closer and closer. I now had some time at home at weekends. I do not remember the name but I was obviously feeling myself again as I took an interest in the young lady who had come onto the ward. She was pretty and great company. We just seemed to get on as we were the only two people on the unit under the age of 40. We also clicked which was nice. My therapy sessions continued in the unit and I was pretty much ready to go. As I mentioned previously, a few days before release day I had to cook lunch for Jim before I was deemed fit to leave. As I stated previously I believe it was a chilli. I hope it was OK but cannot confirm or deny if Jim had finished his. I was very keen to get back home now and the day arrived. I do not recall there being a big hurrah but home I went. I do recall it felt very strange being home and would often return to the unit on the pretence to see this girl. Subconsciously I think this may have been a bit of an excuse as I felt safe at the unit. Please don't allow me to take anything away from the good company of the young lady but I guess the unit almost felt like home. I recall it was nice going back but also felt good to leave on my own terms. I remember the days at home being very long. I was at home alone for large chunks of time and it was not always fun. It did however feel good to be out of the unit. I started trying to increase what I did on a daily basis. This started by walking to the paper shop every morning to get a high-quality red top to read. This is when I made the decision to cross the road exactly where I was hit. I did this and it was not an issue at all. Once I had done it I never thought about it again. I started to take the papers into my local, the Pub I left the night of the bang on the head. This was therapeutic in a way I guess. It also allowed me to speak to somebody I knew face to face. This is something I always enjoyed and still love a walk and the papers today. I am slightly anti-technology as I believe the youth of today will always struggle to chat with people on different levels as you do not learn these skills at the other end of a screen or mobile device. I then branched out and even made it further down the road to Sainsbury's local. As much as I wanted to fill my days I also had to take into account how tired I would get. The day did not need to be very full to make me flat out. The television became a good friend but this made me want more. The only way to improve things is to put yourself out there and get on with things. This being the case I returned football training. At this point, pre tin hat, I could not really join in so I did a bit of running. It has been quoted since my involvement "You did not look steady. It was a bit of a worry". (PAV.) This being the case I stuck at things and got enormous support from the fellas.

I was running around in training and it felt nice to be back around the lads. I tried to find what I would class as a normal existence but being unable to drive and reliant on people for everything made life difficult. The people around me were very obliging but independence was now set as one of my longer-term goals. My recovery was on-going and I was now an outpatient at the Bradley Walsh. In this period of time, I could see progress and hopefully others around me could see some improvements. One of the major things I wanted to do as soon as I got home was to cross the road where I had been run over. I did this at a few different times of the day but to say I was nervous is an understatement. I got over this and to say it was not a big deal is accurate. I would say this to anybody. Often things seem a big deal but when you actually get on and do it you wonder what all the fuss is about. Once over the road I returned to the pub where things had gone very wonky on the 28th August the year before. I went in and spoke with the landlady and this felt normal. It made me think even more that I wanted to return to the normality I once knew. I was now searching for things to try and structure my day as I was now left largely to my own devices. One of the tasks I used to enjoy doing and did more for me than the recipient was to take a paper into the Crown (Local Pub). I was never asked to do this but I always enjoyed trying to be helpful. I am not sure this was but it was greeted with good grace. I continued the rehab as an outpatient and I was in contact with a young lady who was also a patient in the Bradley Walsh. For the final few weeks / month at the unit we had become very close. We were largely the same age and seemed to get on well. I remember her being pretty and we had a laugh. I used to visit her often and maybe things became clouded? I think this was not a good move for either of our recoveries so as soon as it happened it finished. I did not see her again apart from a couple of messages there was no contact. I think this was the early signs that I would always be seeking to do what normal (whatever that is) people my age were doing. This is probably the early signs of some mental weakness / illness which I will happily discuss later. Now things had moved on and the tin hat (titanium replacement to ½ my skull) was all but ready to go. The replacement titanium plate would be screwed to my spine I believe also my jaw and at the front on the remaining skull. This could be inaccurate but it is my understanding. I was now on a countdown to having the replacement surgery. I cannot recall the time frames so I will not speculate. What I do know is when I returned to St George's it was the Monday of FA CUP final week 2007, I thought this was the case but looking at the dates perhaps it was community shield? Serious brain injury! I remember being in the ward at St George's and being a little anxious about the surgery that was imminent. Unlike my first visit to this hospital I can remember sections of my stay. I remember feeling fine about the operation and thinking that the worst that can happen is I don't make it. In reality that was never going to happen but I had worked myself up a bit. I had the surgery and now looked nearer normal. Whatever that is? I am told the surgery was a success and 13 years on I can only assume it was as touch wood everything has gone ok. I remember coming too and being pretty hungry. My family were about and I don't really recall this but I wanted to start talking as soon as possible. Firstly to check I could. I was transferred down to a private room for a day or two and was visited by a friend of mine who was able to come up. He used to play for Spurs and he very kindly signed an autograph for a nurse. I was back on my feet and discharged on the Friday. This allowed me to fulfil another of my goals I had set myself and that was too watch the FA Cup final in the Stoke on Saturday afternoon. I confirmed with the doctors I was ok to have a couple of beers and I arranged to go across. I still had 120 staples in my head and a huge bandage covering the healing scars. I walked into the pub and Deano was on the door he said "I don't even want to ask". I knew Deano from my younger days in Cinderellas when I was a bit louder and arguably a bit of a knob. Deano ran the door and was always very good to me as I don't believe I overstepped the mark too often? Anyway I digress, I went and watched the game in the stoke with some of my mates. This was the first time I could picture myself getting better and back to somewhere close to the life I knew before. From this moment I became very focussed on things and trying to find something resembling normality. I went football training with the fellas and now I was less of a flight risk as I had a head again I joined in and could do a bit more. The fellas were enormously supportive and my touch was OK. I could never tackle and was worse at timing it now. This being the case I was cautious and kept myself to playing at my limits. I received a few negative comments from a few of the fellas although I didn't respond well to one or two of them, after I had calmed down and stopped acting the prat it made me more determined to achieve the best I could. It was now a year after the bang on the head. I was able to be having a pint of shandy in the crown with

Clarky to mark the year anniversary. This was quite a big day. Clarky and the regulars in the Crown were great and it was a celebration of the achievements I had made. This was great and a number of people gave me a lot of their time and best wishes. This was appreciated but only proved a catalyst to keep wanting to achieve more. I was now in a position to re-apply for my Driving Licence. I did this and after a few refresher lessons with my mate Dan (my former football manager), I was back on the road. Dan was great and very gracious as I wheel spun out of the end of my road. Clutch control would take me a couple of attempts. Dad had bought me an automatic Corsa as this was less stressful and tiring to drive than a manual car. My manual car had gone back as I did not continue the payments in hospital. The freedom this gave me pushed my recovery on again and I made huge strides without realising it. This is the part where I didn't fully understand mental health. I was so focussed on making physical strides forward. There was always a new goal I didn't deal with any psychological damage and swept this under the carpet. This will raise its head later in the tale.

Now I had a car, I started driving and it is fair to say that my mates would never have classed me as the best driver in the world and I am pretty sure their opinion would not have changed now I was back on the road. Was I nervous? I would be lying if I said I wasn't. A bit of advice for people, Do not speculate on things that may happen. I did this and worked myself up a bit. If you only deal with what actually exists in front of you it makes life easier and progress is easier to achieve. I got on with things and quickly became more positive and confident. An old boss of mine asked me to come into his new company and do a few days a week at his new start-up company. This was done to help me out. I did this and it continued my development. It effectively helped me in all aspects of life. I was working with people I had worked with years before as they had followed my old boss to his startup. It was a 45-minute drive from home and life felt like it was returning to normal. It meant I was working with an old friend of mine as well. It was nice to work with her again and we get on very well. This helped me as my old bosses bird was still about and she was very nice too. Working with my mate and having these girls around helped me confirm I still appreciated having good banter at work. Please understand the chat came from them not me. I appreciated the interaction with the girls and neither had been struck by the ugly stick. I digress but this sort of thing helped me reaffirm my social standing and how to speak with people on all different levels. I was getting fatter now as I loved a takeaway and I had become lazy as a lot of my energy was put into focusing on work. It was also in my head not to overdo things and I had developed a bit of an attitude that if it was nice and I enjoyed it eat it I nearly died! This was not a good attitude to have and if I am honest is a bit of mental health weakness as you sort of give up on your well-being and appearance.

Now things were getting more back to normal I returned to full time. This was good and a new sales director came in and we became good friends. Now things had settled Mr Clifford put on a do for me which was good. It raised a bit of money for me personally. I also donated some of this to the Bradley Walsh. It was not as much as I would have liked but Mr Clifford insisted a large part of it came to me. Mr Clifford brought some items from Simon Cowell along to auction. We also had a donation from Paul Wellar to auction off. Mr Clifford also brought Bobby Davro along to do a set at the do. He was a very nice fella. Funny and can hold a tune. The evening was a success and 80 friends and family and some staff from the Bradley Walsh attended. All paying to cover the costs of the venue and meal etc. It went well and further helped rebuild myself personally and socially. Was this the time to draw a line under the recovery? In my head maybe it was and in hindsight, this is a mistake. You always have things to improve upon. So life was moving in the correct direction. As with life when we make progress we start getting ahead of ourselves. I wanted to return to NORMAL! I would go to work then at the weekend want to be out with my mates drinking and doing what I always did. This is when mentally I realised I was not quite at my best. Looking back I now understand I was pushing myself too much. I looked at everybody else and I wanted the girlfriend or wife and family life. As I didn't have that I would go out as much as I could. I had a good time but was just masking my unhappiness. I think a lot of people can relate to that and if not addressed will never end well. I got in a spot of bother nothing serious but I dragged friends into a situation they didn't need to be in and I regret that too today. I was cautioned but was being a prat. I was drunk but my inner anger and frustration and feelings that I had been cheated and life owed me. I dragged a few people into things they didn't need to be in and I apologise for that. I wanted to make a change so I gave up drinking and started running again. My mate lived in the flat below me and I started running with his Mrs. This got me into a routine again and made me feel much brighter about things. I guess this is a message for many people. If things are not working make a change. Be positive but it will not happen overnight and you will feel much brighter in the long run.

I was back at work and I was enjoying being back into a routine. I was tired as I had started pushing myself. I was pushing myself both physically and mentally and just had this desire to return to normal and be what I thought I wanted to be. Although I was enjoying work I had come to realise this is not what I wanted to do. The company I was keeping and had worked for in the past excluded I was very aware that I was in a field filled with egomaniac ass holes. I had also realised that although I had some good attributes I was never cut out to go any further in the business. I now knew this. I think Mr Ledger and Trav had always known it but the job I was doing was the most I could ever do. Sometimes it is hard to admit that especially when you're surrounded by good people but admit it to yourself you have too. I made a decision this is not what I wanted to do. I spoke with a friend of mine who was not a close friend at the time more an acquaintance and he suggested I apply for a job at the special needs school he worked at. I thought about it and felt this was something I wanted to do. I was never going to be rich doing this but I didn't know at the time the wealth I would experience from positive outcomes and a sense of well being. The acquaintance became a huge influence in my life and inspired me to continue my recovery. He helped me socially, psychologically, physically by introducing me to Muthai. At this point it is worth saying I am not tough but the technical side and movements massively helped me physically. I applied for the job and got an interview with the head of care. He was a very nice bloke and even though I had no experience gave me a lot of his time. I was also interviewed by the principal of the school. This was another very decent bloke and I felt he had time for me. I was not offered the job my friend and I had originally discussed but the principal saw me more in the classroom so I was offered a job as a teaching assistant. I had never thought of this as a direction I wished to go but after some consideration I decided to take the opportunity. I was still getting very tired at this stage and the school holidays and a break every 4-6 weeks was hugely appealing. I can never thank

Rob enough for introducing me to this as it changed the direction my life took and am convinced for the better. I started work and this is where I would stay for the next five years. I will not take you through this time blow by blow but it was a happy time. I met some hugely inspirational and kind people during and it helped me hugely, emotionally and socially, as for the majority of the time they were very friendly and easy-going staff. A lot of people were very good to me and one person lived fairly close to me and went above and beyond in order to help me out after another small set back. It was a warm spring day at school and it was as ever quite a hectic and full-on day. I was pushing myself more and more both professionally and physically as I wanted to be a lot fitter than I was. I was in a meeting on the top floor of the school and the next thing I knew I was in the back of an ambulance. Rob came with me as I went to the Royal Surrey Hospital. I had had a seizure. My Mum was alerted and met us at the hospital. In short this meant I could no longer drive. My Dad helped / did all the necessary to inform the DVLA. Dad then introduced another thing to me. I had started worrying how I would get to work. I earned money but not a fortune and due to the location there was no way I could have got to site on public transport. Dad had done some investigation and there was a government scheme called access to work. This scheme helped people injured or medically unable to drive receive financial help to get to work by either taxi or public transport. I cannot recall if you needed to be earning below a certain figure but I suspect that is the case. I cannot imagine the government would pay for a CEO to get to work if they had an issue? This was sorted but things were changing at the school. The set back became an issue as my role slightly changed and 2 days a week I worked with the care team which meant I did not finish until 8 o'clock. The school had residential students so we had staff to help look after and entertain the students after school. The person that lived near me used to take me home after the shifts as we worked late on the same day. I cannot thank her enough for this as this relieved a lot of stress that I would no doubt have dealt badly with. I met some great people at the school and worked closely and learned a lot from the head of sixth form. He had been a teacher for many years and along with my friend at the school worked closely with me in how to manage and deal with difficult situations with students. I have an even temperament when it comes to students which is just as well as I had decided education was the direction I wanted to explore. As I said the time I spent at the school was a happy time. The last school year I was there the dynamics started to change. This exposed an area which has been a battle for many years. That is my ability to deal with negative or tricky social or adult work situations positively. I have and did have it for a number of years mental fragility. I would not except this and would never have dreamed about discussing any issues I was having. If anybody has issues TALK. It is not weak but when you learn to do this the areas that are not going well can either be dismissed or worked upon. When you talk this will eliminate the negative thoughts that can cause a snowball of emotion and blow situations up into something they are not. I had a verbal flair up at a member of staff I had clashed with. The long and short of it was the dynamics changing had unsettled me but that is not an excuse, but if I had of addressed it the frustration and negativity would have been quelled. The disagreement was not serious but I did not handle it well and I apologise. I met with the principal and the situation and the school evolving meant I didn't think I should stay. After discussing it I decided to resign and avoid that situation and the imminent changes. I left at the end of term and things had settled by the time I went. I had a positive result at this time. My year of giving up my drivers licence came to an end. I received my licence back and after a few sessions I was back on the road. This made life a bit easier again. The situation at school was easier but because I hadn't dealt with my issues it was time to go. Not my finest hour but the changes had affected me. It was regrettable and at the time a huge issue causing much worry but in hindsight sometimes things happen for a reason?

I then had to find a new job. Some people had said I had been through a lot so chill out. I was not one of those people I always wanted to keep moving forward. I did a couple of jobs away from education that I enjoyed but was never really me. I worked for a year in a parts department at a Mazda Dealership. I met some great people there and had a very nice time working and for the first time since the bang on the head, in an area I could not draw upon past or personal experiences. I say this as although I had no experience in education I had some of the fundamentals that I could relate too and take on advice given to me as some of it came quite naturally to me. I say this as at times I can empathise with troubled people and am generally quite a nice person. There may be a number of people that disagree with that last statement but I hope I didn't upset too many people in my arrogant party boy years. I was pushed in the motor trade as I have no practical or mechanical knowledge and this is something that I really do not understand or learn easily. It took me some time and I asked a lot of questions to the mechanics however stupid I thought they sounded. Thankfully they were happy to treat my stupidity nicely and were happy to explain things to me. My boss who by chance I had played football in the same team the season before the bang on the head was also very supportive. I did not know he worked there until I started and was delighted to find he was my direct boss when I started. This was one of many strokes of luck I had along the way. From my time in the motor trade the piece of advice I would give people is there are no such thing as a stupid question. If you do not know or understand something ask. When you are dealing with a customer double-check details as nobody minds you confirming details however they will get pissed off if they turn up for the goods and you supply all the incorrect fittings / parts. People are decent I find if you work hard and deliver a good service even if you have to double-check some details. Working in the motor trade also helped my recovery socially. I think I am quite fortunate as I like to think I can speak to most people on a number of different subjects. I am always interested in what people have to say and try to take on board anything I am told as it makes you more interesting and will always help you socially professionally and maybe most importantly mentally. I say this as being able to communicate with people and being confident enough to will add to your well-being and make you feel much more positive about things. I had been in the motor trade about a year when I had another setback. I had my licence back. I had had this for a few months and this was making life much easier as I could function much better again. Then the setback hit. I went on a stag do to foreign lands and had a great time. This is another bit of advice I have for people. If you have had difficulties and things are going well do not ditch the positive things you have been doing and get ahead of yourself. I was back drinking. This makes me sound like an alchy but all it means is I was having a pint at football and a couple of beers with the boys maximum once a week. I went on the stag do and apart from sticking to my not drinking when I fly as I was advised medically. I may be fine but alcohol may affect the brain differently in the sky? I did go fairly hard at it. Not really eating no real sleep not drinking anything other than a beer. I had a great time and went with some top people and this was just another reminder to me that I had been very lucky in a lot of ways but things have changed. DON'T TAKE THE PISS SON. I had a seizure on the morning we were returning home so I wound up in an ambulance on my way to BUDAPEST hospital. That was an experience. I had a brain scan which was interesting. In broken English I was also told by a Hungarian neurologist? "A bit of your brain is dead". I was checked over and given an anti-seizure drug and thankfully just made it back on the flight with moments to spare. I must say at this point a massive thanks to my mate Rob who joined me at the hospital and did the awkward phone call to my brother. He was prepared to stay in Budapest with me if we hadn't of made the flight, I would also like to thank Lloyd who remained very calm and knew his first aid and in his words "Pulled your tongue out of your throat" when I was having the seizure. This incident made me feel thankful for the great people I am surrounded by and I always try to stay loyal and would not dream of hanging anyone out to dry. It also made me wake up a bit that I cannot do all the things I think I always did. The truth of the matter is I didn't do them very well when I was young but thankfully never had a serious incident off the back of it. It made me appreciate that I had to live my life a bit better. I saw my doctor and was referred back to the specialist. This was the start of brain scans again. I was once again tested for epilepsy. I was booked to go onto a stag do in Las Vegas 3 weeks after the trip to Budapest. After the seizure funnily for my character in the past I decided myself that this trip was not the correct thing for me to do health-wise. I went back to work at the Mazda dealership but there was something in my mind that said to me I should go back into education. It was arguably the one job I had in my working life that I loved.

I applied for a job at a private prep school which was only ½ mile from my flat. I didn't expect to get anywhere with it as it was supporting a student on a 1-1 basis and in the back of my mind although I had my teaching assistant qualification maybe I was largely under-qualified. In a moment nobody would have predicted I was offered an interview. I went into the school and remembered feeling a little intimidated as it was a completely different setting to anything I had experienced before at my previous school and far nicer than anywhere I went to school many years before. I got on very well with the principal and was invited back a second time which started to give me hope. At this stage I knew the applicants had now been trimmed down to a few. I spent time with a class being assessed on my interaction and was spoken with by a number of SMT staff. Somehow it went well and many years later the principal said it was a huge gamble but one that had worked. He offered me the job. I accepted and although it was June and the start date was September I decided to resign from the car dealership even though my months' notice would mean I was off for August. I was in a position to financially so I decided to give myself a summer holiday and go into the new job well-rested. I still had about 10 months to go on my DVLA ban from driving due to my medical incident. This being the case I continued getting a cab into work. This was supported by the access to work scheme which was yet another thing the state had done for me. To say I was nervous on day one is an understatement. I started and the new setting suited me and I was able to help the PE department and join in when the year group I was working with had sport. My new direct line manager was incredible and over the next five years I would learn many things from her. The student I was working with was a lovely character as was 99 percent of the year group I was working with. The staff were great. I had a lot of time for the principal and the deputy head. They gave me lots of support and in the early years gave me many tips on how Prep schools worked and the dos and don'ts. I was also given a lot of time and great advice from many of the staff. I worked with and met a number of people some of which I hope to class as friends. My favourite year was Year 4. This was a year in and I had finely felt settled and think I was finding my feet. I spent most of my time with the same class teacher. This lady was fantastic and we get on very well and she was a very calming influence on me. I say calming as I was not a lunatic but when I felt lots of pressure I needed a calming influence on hand.

The young man I was working with was needing me a little less by year 5. I spent a lot of my time in the PE department. I think I was Ok at this and if people disagree with that statement I will just have to wear it. I had a lovely time and through ally enjoyed my time with the PE staff. The department was run by the Deputy head Mr Scott who was a fine gent. I learned a lot from him. In the department was a smashing Kiwi, DB and latterly a fella called Alun who temporally ran the department. He was very good to me. There was a fella I really liked who split his time with PE and some other nonsense. As I said I really liked this bloke but referred to him as Numb Nuts, Sloth from the goonies or Barry Evans. This used to wind him up so whenever I walked into the office I would say "Hey you Guys" or "I love you Chunk". Kids stuff but it amused my childish brain and made DB smile as well. In the girls department was STP and Kate. I liked both but got on very well with STP. As time went on I would help out with a number of clubs including football with DB some cricket and Athletics with STP. Football was run by DB and I helped out but found this quite easy as technically I was ok so I found it easy to help out with technique.

DB gave me a lot of his time and helped me as a coach. Cricket I had played and was pretty ordinary so although I could help with some basics was not in a position to bring anybody on. This didn't sit well with me as I wanted to offer some benefit to the children. I wound up speaking with my mates Dad. He had been a bowling coach at county level. He does not suffer fools so I knew I would get it straight from him. He agreed to come into school and do a session 1-1 after school. He walked me through how to coach a good bowling technique. I was working with youngsters so often all that was needed was correct basic technique and let any natural talent take over. He ran me through this and gave me confidence to pass it on. This is another show of the kindness and time people gave me which really encouraged my recovery. This is the time to thank my brother again. As I was spending more time with the PE department I wanted to be fitter and have better coordination and control of all my limbs. I decided to join local fitness classes. I am not sure if Neil really wanted to come but that he did. A big thanks to Carl and Paige at this point. The final club I got involved in was athletics. I know nothing about technique so I was just a body. The reason I got involved was I liked STP and she needed some help. On top of that I was becoming quite keen on running which I will discuss further in the next chapter. As I said I know nothing about good technique for any of the disciplines. I was never any good at school so therefore did not take a great deal of interest. Yet another point for our youngsters or anybody I guess. I often regret not taking a note or giving things my full attention in the past. At that moment in time it means nothing to you. In the future it may become of real use to you. So why waste time, If you are involved in something you might as well give it your all as you never know when it may become of use. As I could not offer a lot I would follow STP lead and provide motivation to the kids and join in to emphasise the instructions given. This didn't sit well with me so I did some research and could now offer some input in certain disciplines.

My time at this school was some of the best years I have ever had in employment. It unfortunately ended five years into my employment. Whilst at the school I had a number of conversations with the principal. He was excellent. He told me he had taken a gamble on me and it had worked. I decided I wanted to move forward and teach. He explained to me that I needed a degree to move things forward. I was academic to a point getting GCSE but no A-Levels. This being the case I did some research and enrolled in an open university Degree in sports fitness and coaching. This is being funded by student loans and at the point of writing this I have completed 4 years of the course. I suffered some mental health issues. Some depression and self-loathing. I received great support but it was time to move on. I will discuss this further in the coming chapters. Whilst at the school I appreciated I was not able to play football. I was never good enough to not try my best to stay competitive. This being the case my injuries and physical limitations and speed of thought made me a problem at training and not in a position to play in matches. The boys never inferred that it was a problem me being about. One dopey comment from a player made me realise what I already knew. It was time to give this up. I did give it up. Now just to categorise one last time. I was of no standard at all. This was reiterated to me by a number of people so I do not want anybody believing I was good. The point in discussing football was it was a big part of my life and is a regret I did not commit or focus properly on it. I spent a number of years helping managers out on match day, run the line etc., but there is only so many years you can be called a cheat and a c*nt every Saturday so I have now stepped back.

My exposure to playing football now was limited to a few years later helping my brothers side out who were short in a vets match. That was fun but never repeated. I had found a new goal and focus. I was going to run.

Running

In the first year of returning home I was bored with just appearing to be getting more and more chunky. I was training with the boys at football once a week but that was not enough for me. I wanted to see what I could do. Before the bang on the head whilst living with my mate, We would run a couple of times after work. I started running a couple of KM. At this point my old school mate who lived in the floor below had just had a baby with his wife. I was chatting and his wife expressed an interest in joining me for a run. For a number of months I now had a partner to run with. This helped me to stick to it and I started to enjoy it again. I had run Reading half marathon and a Nike 10K before the accident so I was not brilliant at it but was not a complete novice. In the middle of the start of my running training I visited a son of an acquaintance of mine in the Bradley Walsh unit. He had a similar injury to me and although a number of years younger than me was having similar difficulties. He was also a lot further back in his recovery. The acquaintance has since become a very close friend. His son wanted to get back to doing something physical as he was a rugby player but not the same level as his dad. We ran a 10K fun run. His lad comfortably beat me around but I believe me saying I would do it helped his decision to sign up. His Dad Grant and I remain very close and run races together. I do beat Grant but he is always quick to point out he is 52 and almost 100Kg. But he does it. His son is a smashing lad and he has rebuilt his life and invited me to his wedding. A very nice family the type of people you need around if you are trying to improve your situation. Post this run and after a few months, I started going out on my own and increasing the distance gradually. As the distance grew I wanted to set myself new goals. This is important as you work on anything. Always have goals. Short-term goals which are achievable. For example try and bring your time down on a distance you consistently run or slightly increase your training routes. Then long term goals. This moment came when by chance I met Rod at the end of my road. I have known Rod since I was about 10. He played at the club my brother played for when he first started playing men's football. Rod will be about eight to ten years older than me but is ridiculously fit. He was doing a training run for the Brighton marathon. He asked if I wanted to join him. I did join him. We were not hanging around and I will be honest it was hard work to keep up. This is the stubbornness I have I was determined I would not turn it in so I kept going with it. Not sure how far we went? I believe it was between 5-7 miles. However far it was? it was about as far as I had run in one hit since the bang on the head. I kept up and enjoyed it. When it was done I wanted to do more. In the coming weeks, I would speak with my brother's mate Jimmy. We decided to run the Windsor half marathon. I now started training properly.

I enjoyed upping the levels of training and adapting my diet. I gave up alcohol whilst I was training. At this stage I was still in the early parts of my recovery so giving up alcohol was easy enough as although I was getting back into a big Saturday night I found it easy to stop it. I think I found it easy to give certain things up and stick to the training because for the first time in my life I was committed. Windsor half marathon came around and I ran it with Jim. We both completed it in under two hours so happy enough with that.

Now things got serious. I wanted to push myself a bit

further. I wound up speaking to Rod and after some conversation we agreed we would run London Marathon. Rod would help me train and it would be a real challenge. By this time I wanted to try and raise some money for St George's hospital. They had saved my life! I approached St George's hospital and got a place through their charity places. Rod is a firefighter and please don't quote me but I believe he had his place through the fire service. Now I had a place for the 2014 London Marathon. I had been running some half marathon races since our initial meeting which was maybe a year and a half previous. I had run a half couple of races with Jim and one with Grant. All the time getting below 1Hr 54. So I had a place and the fundraising started. The important business of starting to plan training came around. It was November 2013 when my place was confirmed. I spoke with Rod and we agreed to start training on January 1st 2014. After some discussion and advice from Rod I decided to follow the same training programme as him. That training programme is the Hal Higdon training programme. I have a friend Dave Nic who has run marathons and he said to me that you are considered a proper runner if you run under 4 hours. This being the case Rod structured our training runs when we met up on some Saturdays and nearly all Sundays to run 8min 30 per mile. Rod would tell me do this and you will run under 4 hours. At the start of training I was pretty much 14 stone. Bit on the heavy side I would say. I spoke with a family friend Brian Hooper (the ex Olympic Athlete) who gave me some dietary tips and the journey began on 1st January. With Hal Higdon you run Tuesday, Wednesday, Thursday Longer run Saturday and longest run Sunday. The Sunday run would start at 6 miles and steadily increase dropping once or twice where you may run quicker until you top out at about 21.5 miles 6weeks before the marathon. Rod got me through these training sessions and I felt ready. There was never any doubt the freak of nature would be ready. We spoke that I would start the race with him and drop off when it was too much for me. I did not want to ruin his race or spoil his time. Marathon day came around and I felt sharp. I was weighing in at 10 stone 2. Hindsight would tell me that is too light for me and you cannot just be skin and bone to complete the marathon well. Rod and I went to the marathon from Woking station. I loved the whole build-up going up to the marathon getting amongst the atmosphere and the start line is just amazing. The atmosphere the nerves and the excitement when starting a half marathon with a lot of people around is impressive. Times that by 1000 and you have the excitement nerves and atmosphere on the start line on London Marathon day. We got started and eventually crossed the start line after 5 minutes of walking shuffling and jogging. The atmosphere was great. Rod and I went off with Rod setting the pace. We stayed together until Tower Bridge roughly halfway. At this point I was starting to drop off so Rod went on ahead. As you cross Tower Bridge some of the elite runners pass you the opposite way. They are 6-7 miles ahead. The speed they are moving at 20 miles into the race is immense. I don't think I can sprint for 20 metres the speed they are going. I kept going my pace had dropped off a bit. Then came the soul-destroying part of the run. It is Canary Wharf. 20 miles in and just the realisation that 26.2 miles is a long way and you still have a decent distance to go. I was run past by this fella, He said "keep going young man". I looked across and said "Sorry mate how old are you?" He replied "70". This inspired me to keep moving. Not at his pace I hasten to add. I got to marble arch and was running on nothing. My body was giving up. It also did not help that it was a hot day. Me and the sun are not friends. My brother says that is the ginger in me. I was really struggling with about 1.5 miles to go then out of a pub appeared my brother, Dan, Clarkey and Gus. I rolled my sleeves up and shuffled the last part of the race. I finished disappointed at about 4hr 25mins. Although I was disappointed not to be under 4 hours and quite a way off the feeling crossing the line was amazing. Then I met up with the St George's people and my mum joined us. I then made the mistake of sitting down. I have had cramp a few times but never like this. I managed with the help of mum to shuffle to the St Johns tent. They massaged my calves and told me to eat a bag of crisps. They said that should get you home. Once I could move we made our way to join the boys at a pub by waterloo station. Rod had gone elsewhere with his lovely wife. The freak of nature had finished in about 3hr 45. I sipped an orange juice and lemonade and have never felt so physically exhausted. A great day a disappointing time but I had done it. I set the goal and achieved it and raised some money at the same time. I had met some friends and my brother, Mum and sister at a bar next to Waterloo station I was over the moon I had done it but it is fair to say I was a little tired. I went back home after a couple of hours in the bar with my Mum ably assisting me on some tricky steps. Once at home I inhaled a Pizza and spoke with a few friends on the phone. I had a call from Dave Nic who seemed over the moon I had done it. He has run the London marathon a few times and was impressed I had completed it. I was suddenly realising that it was a bit of an achievement to complete it and was feeling quite pleased with myself. I was a little disappointed at the same time as I hadn't broken 4 hours and was reminded a few weeks later by Mick, "Well done but you were beaten by a man 10 years older than you by 30 odd minutes". In a way that is a compliment from Michael. He would not have commented if he did not have some appreciation for it. Would this help to inspire me to do more? I was also still a little pissed as Dave had reminded me he did eventually break 4 hours. SMUG GIT! After the marathon, I vowed never to run or train for anything again. I was politely informed by my mate Gus "You will run again you Prat, There will be something that needs money raised for or you will just do it so enough".

Brighton

Now I had the bug. As the year went on I continued to run and after saying I would never run another marathon I found myself contemplating doing it again. It got to the critical time of the year when contemplating marathon entry, September / October. I couldn't shake off the feeling I wanted to do it again. I spoke with Rod who was not as keen as I hoped. I think he was really and we set the wheels in motion to do it again. I contacted St George's probably about the November time and to get Rod and I into the London Marathon looked unlikely. I had failed in the public ballet and was struggling to get a place with St George's. Things were not looking positive.

I guess my advice at this stage to people is sometimes the ideal goal will not always be possible. If this is the case do not just give up and sulk. Look into potential alternatives and if it works DO IT! On this occasion, London was not going to be an option. I had discussions with the Charity team at St George's and they could accommodate us on the St George's team for the Brighton Marathon. I spoke with Rod and we agreed to do the Brighton race. We would raise money again for St George's and we would start training January 1st 2016. Mentally I felt a lot happier once this was done as I now had some focus and was looking forward to committing once again. I will say it again and probably not for the last time I can only thank Rod and his family for all the support I received throughout this. I went to Spain for Christmas to visit my sister and her husband and just to keep ticking over, did a bit of training at their place. I was very fortunate they have a lovely home and I had a nice run to keep my legs ticking over and a gym on-site. January 1st came around again and once back from Spain training started. This is the bit I really enjoy. By eating and drinking the correct things physically pushing yourself I have never felt better. I started collecting some sponsorship on Just Giving and things were now fully underway. Training was done. It went well and I felt good. I didn't put myself under any pressure to break 4 hours publically but in my head, that was always a goal. I had been going for my Saturday breakfasts in the Café were Cem had sponsored me again in food. After a training run Saturday Morning. This would be anywhere from 8 -18 miles I would as often as possible try and meet Dave and family for breakfast. I would have a Lucozade Steak, Bacon, Bubble and omelette and half a bottle of Ketchup. That is a Breakfast of kings. Now race day was approaching. Rod and I went down a week before to the Brighton Hilton to pick up our race numbers. I think it was Easter holidays at school. Picking up the numbers was a great day and on this occasion, I did not make any stupid purchases. Rod told me we would be joined on race day by one of his colleagues from the Fire service who lived Brighton way. I initially thought oh good here we go getting outrun by two people and left sooner rather than later. Rod convinced me this would not be the case. Jono, Rod's mate, turned out to be a smashing fella and on race day Rod drove us down to Jonos house where I met his lovely family. From there we got a short train ride to the start. It was not quite as grand as the London marathon but it had that similar feel about it. There really Is nothing like the atmosphere at the start of a marathon. The anticipation the nerves the excitement and the will to get this started and get this done. At the start we agreed the Pub we would meet in after the race if the three of us got separated and finished at different times. When we were chatting on the way to the start it became obvious that Rod would most likely finish first and it was possible Jono and I would finish in similar times. The Pub was on the seafront so I had an idea how that looked from picking the numbers up. So we were now at the start. The nerves and tension at this point is a strange feeling and you just want to get started.

We started the race together and after a couple of miles, it was Rod and I. This time I stayed with Rod for 15-16 miles and felt quite comfortable. It was a very warm day. I had overdressed for the run and had worn a base layer under my running shirt. After about 9 miles I said to Rod I am burning up. Rod suggested I remove the base layer. We agreed we would do this whilst maintaining on the move. Rod held my T-shirt and I removed the base layer. Before I could get my T-shirt on I had been wolf-whistled. This is the first time this has ever happened and certainly the first time by a fella walking his little dog. I held onto the base layer as My Dad lived near Brighton at the time and I knew roughly were him and his wife Debbie would be watching from. I felt much better now and was stunned I was still with Rod. We continued on the run and whilst in the town it gets a little harder for a stage mentally. You then come out onto the seafront for an extensive run away from town. As you make your way out I managed to settle. We Ran past Debbie and Dad and I am sure they were over the moon when I chucked my sweaty base layer at them. Rod and I continued down the seafront back towards town. You pass the finish line on the other side of the road and we ran past the Pub we were due to meet in. Rod left me now as I could not maintain his pace. You run out the other side of town and then back towards the seafront. You then hit a sole destroying section as you run in and around an industrial estate at about 22 miles. You have to dig a bit deeper at this stage mentally. I was now running alone and kept pushing I looked at my watch and I was doing

OK. Once the horror of the industrial estate is over you are on the final push running directly next to the beach and you start to see the finish approaching. I was dead on my feet but kept pushing 3:59 had just passed. I finished in 4:01. Again I was disappointed but I had cut a big chunk off. Somehow the freak of nature had beaten me by a similar amount as London. Fair to say I was fairly happy with 4:01. Once again I swore I would never run another marathon.

A few weeks after Brighton I ran Hackney half marathon. It started and finished around the Olympic stadium. I was on my own for this one and was very relaxed and no pressure on myself coming into it. I enjoyed the whole race experience and without knowingly pushing myself ran my fastest ever half marathon time at 1:41.

I had a year off running marathons the next year. From memory, I ran a couple of half marathons with Jimmy Russ. He was / Is great support for my running and we have run a number of half marathons together. Our times range from about 1:43 to 1:53. Jim is my brothers mate but he has been very good to me over the years and we are fairly close and I think tentatively he classes me as a friend. I went to watch the London Marathon that year by joining a former work colleague who was running her first Marathon. She did very well. Our friendship came to an end when I left my job. This was in the midst of some mental health issues which I will discuss a bit later.

I had completed a year off Marathon Running, I wanted to do some more and raise more Money. The school I was at through the marathons was the Prep school which I loved being at. The school has an international and UK charity for each academic year. The year of no Marathon I pitched to the students and they selected St George's Hospital as their UK charity. This was fantastic news and the school raised the best part of £9000 for St George's. With the marathons, the massive contribution from Hoebridge School and the football matches the boys had put on specifically for St George's, we were approaching £16,000. The boys had also raised a bit of money for the Bradley Walsh unit for some games in the early days of my recovery. There was also a donation that I made following the charity evening as it felt wrong not to contribute something back. With these the Bradley Walsh maybe received £1500. Please don't quote me on the figures it all gets a bit blurry. I have had a serious brain injury! I think at this point I would like to once again thank everybody who supported me in the early days of recovery and continue to today. I am very lucky to have such great people around me. The boys at the football club would always throw themselves behind any fundraising we could do. Special mention at this point to Gus, Neil, Dan, Stuart Shoosmith and everybody who ever gave up a minute to help me towards raising as much as I / We could. There really are too many people to thank individually Thank you Chippy getting a side together to play as they were the two teams I used to play for Saturday and Sunday. Whilst mentioning Chip it is the correct thing to do that in the early days if my recovery fellow QPR fans Chip and Rum took me to some games at Loftus Road. THANK YOU

So I had got to a reasonable amount of money and I wanted to do as much as I could. I had it in my mind I wanted to get to £20,000. I would never hit that amount but got quite close. I had a year off the Marathons and after going up to watch and still feeling quite fit as I ran some half marathons it made me want to do it again. The atmosphere and the energy around the start line was incredible. This being the case I spoke with St George's and the freak of nature and we agreed to run Brighton then miss a week and run London. I then signed myself up to the Milton Keynes Marathon a few weeks after London and Liverpool Marathon a week later. I would not make that as I was not in the correct place mentally to push myself that much. I will explain this in the coming chapters. So Rod agreed to do it and St George's would back us. We now had places for both Marathons and it was the end of November. We pencilled in starting to train on the 1st of January again. The normal restrictions would apply. No drinking, correcting my diet, No caffeine and generally good living. The training was going well and was very much needed as this is the period of time where things began to get on top of me mentally. I will discuss this in more detail shortly. For now I will concentrate on the running. The training was tough and I think mentally the thought of doing 4marathons in 5 weeks was weighing heavy on me. I got to about the start of March when the pressure got too much. I dropped Milton Keynes and Liverpool and would just focus on the two races. Rod continued to help me around the training runs and I felt ready although there were some doubts as I had lost the determination to push on having to walk on the 21-mile training run. RUBBISH! So Brighton marathon day came. In my head, I had been unwittingly putting pressure on myself to run both races under 4 hours. That was a bold call and I would not get under 4 hours. Rod and his lovely wife would once again make sure I got down there and this year it was just Rod and I at the start. It was another warm day but this time I was more appropriately dressed. We started and it was a good start with a big sense of relief that it was here. I ran with Rod for about 8-9 miles and he was moving too quick for me so I let him go. He is a machine and has the drive without any fuss that I have not really seen from anyone else. So I was not in the most comfortable running rhythm but kept pushing on. Saw my Dad at about 11 miles which gave me a bit of a lift. I was now running back down the promenade. I ran past the pub that I would meet Rod and his Mrs in. This gives you another lift as you start thinking of the finish. Then something happened that I never believed in before. I hit the wall. I believed up until now that it is something people said when they were underprepared and just didn't have the ticker for it. I had run past a few people receiving medical treatment on the side of the road one gent, in particular, looked to be in real trouble. The macho rubbish in me likes to think this didn't affect me but I think it may have. I started to walk at about 19 miles. At this point, I was questioning why I should do this. I have nothing to prove I have done this before. I was very close to giving it up. At this stage a fella whose name I didn't catch or probably more likely I cannot remember wound up walking with me for about ¼ mile. We chatted and without realising it he refocused me. We agreed to run together we did this for a while but he is was in much better shape and he went ahead. I had been through the what's the point motion as the time looked to have gone. But after our chat, I just thought that is not important. What was important was not giving up and letting down the people who had kindly sponsored me. My pace was not brilliant but I was adamant I would not walk again even through the soul-destroying industrial estate. I got through the industrial estate and was now on the seafront. This is when another lift occurred. I was in a group of 3 or 4 and we ran towards some spectators. They seemed fairly convinced it was Fatboy slim if it wasn't he looked a lot like him. Not sure why this gives you a lift but it did. Now just over a mile from the line. This really hurt but dug in and ran past the pub we were meeting in. Finished in an initially disappointing 4 hours 25. After I realigned and got over myself that my time was not what I wanted I made my way to the pub.

This is something I learnt when I had to get myself mentally happy. It is unrealistic to put yourself under pressure to get to a level you may not. I was not a professional athlete I had just completed 26.2 miles get over yourself and enjoy it. I went and met Rod and Gill in the pub and Rod had done a ridiculous time best part of an hour ahead of me but I had done it and not given up when I was close to doing so. This is a life lesson for people that may help. Don't always compare yourself to others sometimes celebrate what you have achieved. Use others accomplishments to inspire you to do better but do not beat yourself up as a failure. I had used Michael to inspire me to go again. Rod seemed impressed that we had both completed it again. We had a nice afternoon in the pub, I stuck to the orange juice and lemonade the caffeine was my treat. The freak of nature had a few beers. We still had London to run.

The week in between I did some low-level training just to tick over and met Rod in the middle Sunday to run 7-8 miles just to tick over.

LONDON was here. Pressure off the under 4 hours for all runs was not an option. Just go and enjoy it. Once again the journey up from Woking station is some of the more enjoyable parts of the day. The train is full very early on a Sunday morning most decked out ready for the run. We got up there and the experience was much the same; we joined the almighty cue for the toilets dropped off the gear decided which pub to meet in after then onto the line. We were underway and with the pressure off I really enjoyed the opening 4-5 miles. I let Rod go just before Tower bridge and settled into a rhythm. I didn't have the issues with Canary Wharf this time. I just kept going and crossed the line in 4 hours 9 minutes so missed out again. I got my medal and no need to visit the medical tent this time. I walked off to meet the St George's team Rod and Gill and a few others who had been of great support at the Pub. There was no running to be done now so Rod and I sat down for a pint. Pressure off and a very enjoyable afternoon. Goes without saying Rod had run quite close to 3 hours 30 again. So the marathons are done. Never been under 4 hours and just shy of £20K but that is it. At the time I wrote this I am 41 at the end of the year I am too old, so that is it. Or is it? No, it really is. It turns out they are quite painful.

Image of Rod and me after London

Mental Health

This is the area of my recovery I never really took into consideration. I was so focussed on getting it correct physically and more than happy to take the plaudits and positive comments from my mates if I did something well at football or ran another race. That was all that mattered to me. It turns out the mental side of my recovery would be a much tougher nut to crack. And if you do not monitor it things can reoccur in the future. As I have stated before, the recovery went well and I made huge visible strides quite quickly. These are the obvious areas to the outside world as with all mental issues the patient will often suffer in silence and not allow their fragility to be exposed. Now this statement makes it sound like I was tortured mentally for all the years of my recovery. This is not the case. I had found that setting myself short medium and long term physical goals had given me a focus and a purpose. This is a good tool for anybody to use when trying to structure their life and give them purpose. The drive that is needed and the delight achieved when you achieve your goal is well worth the tough training needed to get there. I am talking a physical goal but any individual suffering can change the direction their life is going by working towards short medium and long term goals. Now this is where it is important: You must not get so blindly focussed on achieving the platinum level of your end goal. I felt disappointment at the end of the marathons. I had not run under 4 hours. I was shy of raising £20K for St George's hospital and I had not run 4 races in 5 weeks. This brought me down massively. I was already at a low Ebb at this time which I will discuss shortly but this added to my poor state of mind. It is important for you to celebrate the achievements you have made and not beat yourself up about the could of would of should of. You have achieved more than you could of at the start of the journey so you as a person and potentially the organisation you are working with or for are much better off than when you started. This being the case, celebrate the achievement. You must do this even if you did not fully get to your desired end goal. You must set yourself a tough end goal at the start because what is the point of making it easy. This goal may not have been possible and always just out of reach but you will get so much further if you originally reach for the stars. Being disappointed I didn't break 4 hours at the end of it all was healthy because it proved I wanted it. What is not healthy is to dwell on this and beat yourself up. Use reflection, admit it is disappointing but also reflect on where you started and how far you have come and learn to celebrate and accept that. This is also a time not to compare yourself to others. You can always use others for inspiration but for a time I would compare myself to others and feel like a failure as I did not break four hours. It is vital that everybody learns to accept the level they have achieved. If you can look at yourself and say I did everything I could to get there but just fell short you just need to be prepared to go again.

Me personally now. I was interested largely in getting back to how things used to be for a large part of my recovery. I was happiest when I was in situations that after a while seemed natural to me as it was the circles and life I knew. This is a good mental lesson for people. Admit to yourself that maybe you want to change things. If you keep fighting against it and masking it, putting yourself in familiar situations it will only add to the distress. If you cannot admit that life has changed and things that are important have moved on you will always struggle. For me, a lot of years had passed and my friends had grown up and started getting married and everything was settling down. I didn't understand this but it became apparent that is the way I wanted my life to go. Now when you can finally admit to yourself there are issues address them. I say this as another problem I always had historically was managing money and saying no to a night out if I couldn't afford it. This became a big issue as the value of money continued to mean nothing to me and after being left to manage things myself. I proved I had learned nothing on this front and I wasted a large amount of money. Always chasing something but didn't know what? And masking the unhappiness I felt. I would not admit to myself or see the problems I was causing. I was always trying to please all the people all the time. The truth is looking back I didn't need to as I was getting on fine and nobody expected anything from me. I had such a self-loathing that I wanted to do all I could to make sure I fitted in. As I said in hindsight this was never needed as I have a great bunch of mates. Once you are in this spiral in your own mind however things get you always feel inadequate and think you should have done more. Things get into a spiral and before you know your situation is becoming unmanageable and you do not see it you are just filled with self-doubt and your influence or existence has no real purpose or significance. It is vital at this time that you do not try and solve everything. You must address one issue at a time and by doing this the self-doubt and feeling of isolation will start to disappear without attacking it directly. I have never spoken about this to anybody close but when you say it out loud you realise it is not an accurate viewpoint. I wanted to change but I needed help to do this and keep me ticking along for a period of time. I was fortunate that my Brother and Dad were on hand to help me out when things got to a very worrying time. My Brother stepped in and gave me some cruel to be kind words and this was the catalyst to change my ways. This did not happen instantly and I had to get to the very depths to start to rebuild. The support I received was key. I guess what I am trying to say is to get an individual out of a bad and often dark place you cannot do everything for them. You must let them try and then want to come out the other side. Once they want the support it is, hopefully, there and I would hope progress has been made. The aim for the person coming from the dark place should not be wanting people to be proud of you but to not be a burden and enjoy living a normal life enjoying things and not having one area of your life being the first topic of conversation. That mantra can cover a number of aspects of life. Change who you are so it does not define you. It may take time but it is worth getting to. From there you can start to enjoy living your life and focus on other areas. It is important to understand that the changes you believe need to be made may not be as drastic as you feel they need to be. Do not change everything you are, Enjoy yourself but growing up may be what is required. You are you just try and become a better version. I am always changing and growing up. I am better than things were previously but you will always change and you can always grow. Effectively you are always working progress. It is almost impossible to set a long term goal for your emotional and mental health as the dynamics will constantly change. This being the case, work off short and medium-term goals, work hard to be the best version of you. Have fun and life will be much brighter. A person at the lowest will see no way out and they will constantly try and mask their failings. If you are ever helping somebody and things get to the lowest ebb please never say that an action is a cry for help. This could not be further from the truth. When I was at my lowest it was not a cry for help it was taking some control on what I felt was a hopeless situation and not seeing a way through this. I had some empathy and managed to bring myself back by thinking of the people around me. This started the latest road to recovery I was on. You cannot always solve things for people. Be there but the person themselves needs to want to get better. I did and that journey has been hugely rewarding. Another huge issue I had was always wanting to be liked by everybody. I had this horrible feeling that people always pitied me and I was never really anyone's equal. I wanted to be like everybody else and NORMAL. I don't like that word but what does it mean? When you are struggling this can mean your perception of how wonderful everybody else life is. Always having that feeling that people are looking down their nose at you or pitying you. This takes many years to get over in my experience and I still have moments when I feel beneath people, inferior and just not accepted. The important thing I have learned is that there are many different people in this world. Hopefully, you can surround yourself with the good people and in time you will learn to care less about the bitter, always having a pop type characters. It took me many years to not let the anxiety these people can cause and the fear of the anxiety that may be caused not to be a real mental health and emotional disorder. I did not feel I fitted I always felt I was below people and behind closed doors away from the world I spent a lot of time feeling very low. There is no magic switch to turn this off and like everybody else I still need to deal with negativity towards my actions or character. Unlike before I can now work with this and do not need the reassurance of everybody to get my head together. People who are negative or have an air they are above you can be tough to deal with. Be happy with yourself and unless the points made are very valid and useful to help you move forward try not to react. I by no means am perfect I still have a number of flaws but with support and the desire to become more chilled socially and not as regimented, I continue to make small progress. Ask Phil and Clarkey: I am not chilled I like a structure. I think it drove them to distraction when we were away on holiday, but they were very gracious and I think I learned a few things about myself and how to relax a little bit. There is no switch when you are battling anything, so when mentally you are struggling it can only ever be measured in small steps and you must not become so focussed on long-term goals. Hit the short and medium-term goals and when you relax and let things happen (much like looking for love) things happen in their own time. In recent times during the pandemic, I have struggled mentally. My life is in a good place but I am putting myself under increased pressure as I want to better myself and have a better life for my partner and me. It has recently come to a head and I have started meeting with a counsellor remotely to discuss my low mood and because I am quite relaxed normally I have obvious increased anger and anxiety. From the sessions I have had I have suffered from the lack of routine because of the pandemic. My lack of social interaction and anything which has made me feel vulnerable or scared / anxious has brought back my feelings of being in hospital. This is when I was anxious of the future not in control of my own destiny and being told what I could and could not do. I had no real control over my routine as is the case as we skip from lock down after lock down. This has led me to want to be liked and please everyone. I have become the great pretender. Not telling anybody how I really feel playing a number of different roles in the hope to please all the people all the time. I had just felt anxious lonely lost and scared. When I have stepped back from this and discussed it with the counsellor and my partner I realised these emotions are not unusual and are not the same as being in hospital. If you discuss your issues you can nip the anxiety and stress that is being caused in the bud. I hope to keep making improvements and instead of worrying about ifs buts and maybes, deal with what is in front of me. Take some of the advice I have given students in the past. Worry about what is in front of you. It is not weak to ask for help. It is weak to put on a mask and just hope it will all turn out fine. Pressure and stress will build the anxiety and this can spiral quickly. Be true to yourself and speak to people. Things are hard at the minute don't wish for things that cannot happen. Don't panic about what the future holds. None of us knows how this plays out. Find ways to ease the stress. I recommend going for a run and talking to those close to you. They will not judge you they will want to help you. Often when you say it out loud you can defuse the issue quickly and dismiss a lot of your worries.

We are in a pandemic at present and I am aware a lot of people may be struggling with Anxiety and depression. I have started to struggle at times as I have been taken back to when I was in hospital emotionally and mentally. I have felt helpless and situations are out of my control. I don't feel settled therefore I do not feel people A) like or accept me or B) I need to impress or seek approval by setting tough goals for myself. Adding hugely to the pressure and stress but trying to find common ground and acceptance. I am aware a lot of people are really struggling at the time of the pandemic so although I am not comparable please talk. This will help and hopefully break the cycle of despair and anxious thoughts. Do not speculate or look too far in the future. Have short term goals and keep them to yourself or those very close so no pressure is added in your mind from the outside.

Emotionally

Emotionally my recovery was a rollercoaster. In the early days, I did not experience any negative emotions as I was quite driven. I was driven without really understanding what I was driven to or what I was capable of achieving so everything was a bonus. It did not matter how small the step was it was positive. This is where I believe it is possible to set yourself short term targets and longer-term targets. When setting these targets, do not make them reliant on the input of others. You cannot effect the actions of others so do not put this pressure on yourself. Emotionally I struggled as I never felt good enough for anything and had very low self-esteem and felt like I was being judged on everything I did and said and in my depression and anxious phase I would always imagine that everything was worst case. I have a bit more of an understanding on mental and emotional health and in my younger days I would say "Pull yourself together" and all you need is some straight talking. There is room for some real and straight talking but it is an illness and I understand how this can snowball now. You must realise it yourself and talk and understand the issues. This is now the time for some structure and actions have consequences talk as you now have the ability to process it. You cannot just snap out of it and stop seeking that reassurance from those around you. My circle of friends and family was great but it is a lonely fight. You need to get to the point you want help and are prepared to be happy again on your own. I had hit a very low ebb emotionally as I did not ask for that help. I say this as one of the biggest issues I had was feeling bitter about the time I had missed out on and how different my life should be. There is no point looking back and feeling you should have achieved more. This came to a head when I was at the job I loved in the prep school. I felt I was at an age where I should have a wife be settled with a house and a nice family life. I was unaware of mental health at this point and did not realise how not discussing something can put you in a lot of emotional distress and cause huge mental discomfort and worry. I had made some decisions which for a number of circumstances had put stress on my situation I was now struggling with these and burying my head in the sand. For example why had I changed my car a few times and lost a vast amount of money doing so. Why did I have to spend to excess? This was causing some emotional discomfort as things were strained with some important family relations. Dad and my brother helped me understand that actions have consequences. Money and me overspending on stupid cars and searching for something was my main problem. I had also fallen out with a female colleague who I had quite a good friendship with. In my mental distress maybe I felt she was going to ease the burden mentally. This is where things can get clouded you can find yourself making nonsense scenarios in your mind which will make things ok. I had this some cock and bull rubbish about masking my other misgivings and everything would be ok. If we were friends again it would ease my pain. When things turned sour and me not living within my means came to fruition I took a big downward turn mentally. It culminated in things getting very very dark and me feeling at rock bottom with no way out. I apologise to anybody I may have treated poorly at this time. I thank my friends and family for helping me get through this dark time. I thank the support I had from Mr Scott, Mr Arkell and many others at the school. Mrs Campball, Joyce, Mrs B, DB, Numb Nuts, Hayward and Mrs Miller and Clive also need a mention. I left this job as it was the right thing to do. I had not behaved brilliantly and it was obvious I needed to help myself. I loved working with the students but the dynamics had changed and it was correct for everybody to move on. Often it will take a defining moment to accept you need some help. If you can avoid this and have the ability mentally to recognise that you need help speak with people and the problem will ease. There is no disgrace in asking for help either within your circle or professionally. I had been fed back into the medical system which I was initially opposed to as I went through the emotion of I am not weak or nuts. You are neither of these things. The first time you are strong again is when you accept you need some help and allow yourself to embrace it. I spent some time with my GP Dr Guard who continues to be a great, support although I don't need him in the same capacity these days. From there I was referred back to the care of St George's hospital as an outpatient. I attended the Wolfson Neuro-Rehabilitation Unit for a number of weeks and managed to work through the issues that I had been having. I could start to rebuild any personal relationships that had become strained and life looks better. Admit to yourself that you need some help and once you have it embrace it. As I said if you think something is missing and you are continuously looking for it you will never find it. It is not in your control and when it doesn't come you can only find yourself getting more emotionally distressed. I had achieved what I wanted to and run marathons I now just needed to be thankful for what I had and I started to feel a lot happier. I think if I am honest I was a little lonely. My friends were always around as was my Mum but I was envious of the family units some of my friends had built. Do not get transfixed on wanting something as you are not sure what you want so it just causes more turmoil. Live your life the best you can exercise and do not try and cover anything missing with something else. It will not end well. In my case, the cover emotionally was spending money which I didn't really have. I have sorted this now with some straight talking from a few who made me appreciate this cannot continue. In my situation, I need some tough love to make me understand that the way I was doing things could not continue and had repercussions. Dad and Neil did this although tough at the time I appreciate it immensely. I had the constant support no matter what from Mum. This is vital as you never felt on your own. There was some sound, non-sugar-coated advice from my brother in law. "You can't do that you C*NT". The point I am trying to make is that in my situation I required the input from all to help me understand it was time for change. It refocussed what was important emotionally and settled my mental state and anxiety. I stopped me feeling sorry for myself - is not fair I almost died. Do not make excuses. Tackle your issues. Mental and emotional health has and like for many will remain a fight. Take on board the tips you are given and do not stop doing the correct things. Talk and be honest with yourself always. Never think I don't need to do this I am fixed. Anxiety and frustration will creep up on you!

Relax and stop looking and inevitably things will happen. I stopped looking and along it came and I am very happily engaged and own a house with my Fiancee and have never been happier. Could I have seen this 4 years ago? Not a chance. Relax do things better and with a tailing wind it will happen. Do not push it, Put yourself out there to make progress and see how it goes. The main thing I learnt from the darker times in my recovery is it is not weak to talk. The weakness is not accepting something is bothering you, Masking it by just getting on will never deal with the issues. I managed to address my issues but had to allow it to go very much the wrong way. Be strong admit any distress earlier and work your way back - TALK. For many years after the accident, I was very precious. I would take things to heart. I would always see a bit of fun as a personal attack. I am much better now but my ability to not care what anybody thought of me will pop its head up if I do not keep doing the correct things. I surround myself with good people and have good friends that have helped me along the way. Dave has been great as ever. Gus and Neil have been great influences as has Martin my Brother Jimmy Russ and Grant. I have had some great holidays with Phil, Clarkey and Dan who have put up with my structure. Do not surround yourself with people who will just blow smoke and tell you what you want to hear. People who you can have a laugh with but will help you appreciate things in the correct manner are the people to be around. If things have gone downhill in life, the people you need will always be around. Life and the world change. You do not need to see somebody all the time to know they care. A sign of a true friend is for you to always have the best of intentions for them and them for you. This means you don't have to see them all the time but when you do everything will be as it always was. Am I perfect? Absouloutly not but that is OK. Can I say I have addressed some issues and have a more balanced look and not bitter. Yes but it is always work in progress and that's OK. Perfect is never the goal because it is not realistic. Be you be happy and be healthy. Issues are not always obvious like drugs or alcohol. My emotional distress was often masked. At this time especially be nice to people and try to help. When the individual is ready for that help they will become less selfish and hopefully help themselves.

At this point, a huge thank you to Anna and Dave who made me godfather to their lovely daughter. It was a number of years ago, about 11, and I have not been as good as I should have been. I had some battles to fight and hopefully, I have won a few of them. I understand you will always keep improving so it is working progress. I now intend to be much more visible as it is a huge honour to be trusted with that position. I thank you for that and will endeavour to do a better job in future.

Back to Work

So I was now looking for a new school to join. I joined a very nice primary school on the other side of Guildford. I was a teaching assistant in year three initially. This was tough as I had not been with students that age for some time. It was very different from the prep school I was previously at but that is ok. You should never look back as this can be negative to anybody mentally. You can appreciate what you once had and work hard to get to a level you want to be at once again. I enjoyed my time at the school but was also working in the after school club to make up my money. This made the role feel a little disjointed and it was a very long day. I moved into year 6 where I was better suited after ½ term and once again I enjoyed it but it was a long day and a split role which I was finding difficult. I was forever rushing to make any of the fitness classes which were hugely important to me. This school was just what I needed and although I was only there for a term I hope I did OK? As it was becoming stressful trying to juggle everything I started looking for another role. As of the time of writing this book, I applied for a role in a secondary school and this is the role I still hold. This was initially a daunting prospect as I had never had any dealings with students of that age. I got the job and was very taken and impressed by the assistant head and Head as I was shown around and then interviewed. As I said I still work there today. It is a great school full of great staff who have developed what I know and how to approach certain situations. I am not perfect so can always learn new things. I have always had a bit of a snap since the bang on the head. Raised voices and direct instruction works a lot of the time with younger students but not always with the older ones. I have learned many new approaches from the fantastic staff at this school. I guess my message here is if things are not how you want them do not just react, think long and hard ask for some advice and if the answer is change it - DO IT! Surround yourself with good people. I have done this with my friends and have been lucky that it has happened naturally at work. They have helped me develop and now I have the drive back to achieve as much as I can. As of writing this, I am now four years into an Open University degree and once I have a degree I would potentially like to enter into teacher training. I would say it is unlikely I will stay at this current school. If you cannot stay somewhere to achieve your goal you must be prepared to change things to achieve any of the goals you have set yourself. At any time it is not weak to ask for help. I am in no rush to start my new goal. I say this as do not overload yourself. This will cause stress and you must be balanced before you start tough end goals. I could list so many names of people who have inspired me at this school so I will not as I am bound to miss somebody. The head and the SLT are always available to chat to if you need any advice as is my direct line manager Mrs Dawes and the top SEND boss Mrs Cullen. All of these people have helped me along the way and hopefully grow into a better member of staff. It is important to admit if you have a weakness. I have admitted I am not great at some things so I have had support then you move forward. Be honest with yourself and others. If you're not great at something admit it and work on it. Not Weak. It is honest and you will be happier and live life with a smile. Anyway, I have managed to continue some of the coaching which has been a joy and for me moving forward in the future have received some great examples and advice from a number of people. Mr Wright has been great to me and let me have some input to a PE lesson rather than just supporting, He has also allowed me to work with smaller groups which has improved my confidence especially as the age group was new to me. He also gave me some excellent advice on the delivery of the lesson or the training points. All the staff without exception have a lot of time for you and if you work hard which I hope I do you will get something back. I hope I have developed trust and the staff have some confidence in me which allows me to do more which continues to improve my development. I guess what I am wittering on about here is whatever you are doing whether it be a new job or career, university coming back from mental health issues or any other scenario I have missed. You only get out what you put in. If you set yourself short term goals working towards longer-term goals. Work hard try and absorb advice and guidance along the way. If you work hard people are more likely to invest some interest in you. Now this sounds like I think I am perfect. I am not I have many floors but I will say I try and always work hard. I have surrounded myself with good people, They get me. I have some things I still can get wound up by now and again so I know I just need to chill the f*ck out for a few minutes and reset rather than push on through. I am fairly mild-mannered but need to reset from time to time. So not perfect, happy to admit it. I am no danger to anybody but you always have to work on being the best version of you. So I have been lucky I love my job and life now is very good. It has been a bit of a journey.

The journey continues, I am happy to say that I am settled but it is important that everybody remembers you are always learning. I will walk into lessons with maybe 20 different teachers a term. I cannot try and copy anybody you must be your own person. In any scenario or walk of life, you can model certain parts of yourself on the positive impacts people have on you. It is important to remember you will never know everything you are always learning. I enjoy this journey as from where I started I have learned and appreciated the opportunity that is in front of me. If I had some of this outlook when I was younger should of could of would of. Wherever you come from whatever situation you are in, make the best of things. Set some goals to improve the dynamic of your situation. You may not get there but let's give it a good go. It is important not to look far into the future and picture scenarios that may never happen. Do not put this stress and pressure on yourself. Keep your hopes and dreams close to you and this will illuminate a lot of pressure as you are only working for you. When you publicise everything you are doing it adds pressure. You do not need to tell the world in order to feel excepted but work for you and fate will dictate.

When I was working in IT as a young man. A customer of Parkies who I supported would always sign his emails off in a certain fashion. His name is David Rabson (Rabbo). A very fine gent who always had a lot of time for me. He made the effort when I first had my accident to keep up to date with my progress. He is also friends with Howellsy and his brother Gareth who have also been great to me. That being the case inadvertently are paths may cross. Anyway, I digress: Rabbo would always sign his emails off with I thank you kindly BE ALL YOU CAN BE. This is the title of the book as this now means a great deal to me. At the time I would roll my eyes and say something less than witty when I read that. Now it means a lot. I took it on board. I now want to work to achieve all I can with what I have. This message can relate to anybody from any background or situation. If you want something only you can achieve it. Nobody will do it for you, do what you need to, in order to get you to a position to achieve all you can. The only person who can help you start the process of Being ALL YOU CAN BE is you.

I want to say it one last time in this section If you have fears, worry regret, secrets burning a hole inside you do not suffer in silence it will never get better. Talk to someone surround yourself with good people and influences and do not bury your head in the sand. It will not go away it will only get worse. Often the worst case you have in your mind is nowhere near the reality. If it is, work hard and get yourself out of it. TALK TALK TALK. Ask for help.

Life Now and The Future

So as I said I am working in Hinchleywood Secondary School which I absolutely love. I am very happy and engaged. This came when you stop constantly looking and having a picture in your mind of how things should work out. The lady I am engaged to is brilliant and quite possibly the nicest person I have ever met. More importantly, she gets me. This is a great feat in itself as very few get me. I like to think I am Kind and she often tells me I am but she has helped me become a better version of me. The main thing that we get correct is we just get on! Anyway, I digress. I am lucky as I am very happy with life now. Now we got together when I stopped setting goals and putting pressure on where I wanted to be and what I wanted to achieve. You can only set goals on scenarios you can control. Meeting someone getting along and if you're lucky falling in love is out of your control. This being the case you cannot affect your mental health by putting pressure on this. This is a time to continue to put yourself out there. Take a chance may be at times and just be yourself and let things develop naturally. Do not force things but react to the moment and build a life. When you can stop putting pressure on yourself you will not add to any depressive thoughts you have if in the back of your mind you still are not where you want to be. Be honest with yourself. If things are not quite right do not stick with it to try and fill the gap and take you closer to the end goal. This will not help you mentally. This applies to anything in your life. If you are struggling with your weight which I have. Roll your sleeves up and do something to get yourself to nearer where you want to be. If your job is not what you want look to change it. Do this in a proper manner as snap decisions will cause more heartache. Anyway, I will get off my soapbox but one thing I have learned over the last few years is the only person that has full control of your personal wellbeing is you.

So now that I have wittered on I will continue with the tale. At the time of writing this, I am due to get married within the next 12 months. We have come out of one lockdown but back into a second full national lockdown through Covid-19 and I hope a brighter future is ahead of us? I will not discuss the future on these two subjects much more as I do not have full control over how they will progress. I cannot pressure myself with this as I can only do the best I can do and hope these factors work out well. That said I do have a bit more control over the wedding so I will continue to try and help as much as I can and it is fair to say I am very excited about what is to come. I never thought I would get to this situation in my life. It is a nice feeling to have been at a fairly desperate time at different periods over the last ten years and worked through the different challenges. I have been helped by many people and I can only once again thank the huge lengths my family and friends have gone to, when helping me through any psychological issues. Do not think you can stop doing the correct thing when you feel better. If you do not keep talking and working through issues it can come back to bite you at any time.

These have taken many guises and nothing has made them give up on me. I have had to take some ownership too and hopefully moving forward I can continue to be a better version of me and be happy. I think the main thing that has helped me is not only thinking of yourself. A few years ago I would evaluate how certain behaviours would affect others and this helped me rectify and become less selfish. Now I have somebody very special with me who I always think about in any decision I have. If you are not yourself mentally it is a lonely selfish existence. You must let others in to help and you will make huge strides forward.

Moving forward I will continue my degree. I hope to finish in the next year or two and then I will evaluate where I am and try and move my career on. This goal is to move my career on. I have not got too far ahead on this as circumstances and opportunities may change so I will not pigeonhole myself on one particular career path. Something I have learned over the years is not to put too many fixed, long-term goals that require the input of others. By me saying my career needs to go in a particular way and at a designated pace and time is almost setting yourself up for failure. You can have ideas of best-case but must be open to change and adapt. When there are a number of variables out of your control you must be willing to move the goalposts slightly but maintain your drive to succeed. Moving forward I will continue to deal with some areas that still cause me frustration but I must learn to live with. At times I still feel a little bitter at what I think I may have missed out on in the years I was recovering. This is not a huge issue now at all but I have learned to deal with it. I look at my life and for the things I think I missed out on I remind myself what I have. What I can do, What I have achieved and how different that may have been. Without even thinking at the time of the accident the thought of playing Golf would be beyond my physical capability. I was never very good at all but Rod and Andy have invited me along with them and I have had a great time. Just for the record, I was always awful before and I remain consistent. Anybody can do this as they progress their life forward from a difficult time. Look at the potential worst case of the situation you were in. Draw on the positives that you have achieved and look to the future with your glass half full rather than half empty. I think it is very important to keep physically active for peace of mind. I still run a bit and when the world is open I love circuit training and Body Pump. Thank you to all who have helped me along the way with these. I still get frustrated that at times when speaking or writing I cannot think of the correct word or saying. It is there but my brain just cannot process the word. This for a time used to make me a little angry and in a way upset. Now I can smile take a minute and hope it comes to me. If it doesn't I will try and use a different word or structure the sentence in a different way. I can do this now as I looked at this problem and rather than feel bitter I looked at the worst-case scenario. Being able to read write and structure sentences verbally at one point was not guaranteed. Now at times I may stutter or lose my chain of thought but this is on minimal occasions. I have a lot to be thankful for and I just need to keep working at things. As I said this happens fairly infrequently now but is still noticeable to me. The other two areas I get frustrated with at times is physically I may have an issue from time to time. I may struggle with some coordination on my left hand side which may affect my ability to catch a cricket ball, Strike a football with my left foot or jab with my left hand when punching the pads. This is something close to my heart as the concentration it initially took to do was huge. After a time, the movements became more fluid although I still hit the pad like a 90-year-old woman. I would stand there sometimes if I dropped the ball, misplace a pass with my left foot in coaching with the students or punch a pad weakly and think if it hadn't been for that accident Oh woe is me. Now let's be honest. Before the accident, I could not catch a cold when I played cricket. I would possibly hold 1 in 3 at a push. I never used my left foot when playing football and I could not punch my way out of a wet paper bag. I guess the point I am making is when you are coming back from something physically or mentally do not have a distorted view of how you believe you were before. If you measure any progress against a distorted view of the past and where you started from you are always setting yourself up for failure. If you are working on anger mentally you cannot go from being Mike Tyson to Graham Norton instantly just because you are working on things and made some progress, It will take some time but stick with it. You will get there. The final thing that remains a frustration is on occasions I may struggle with my processing of a number of instructions. This does not affect me in the classroom or on the sports field. I think this is because often this comes more naturally to me. This could be trying to structure a day out or people meeting somewhere. I think this drives people to distraction as I must plan things to the minute in order to settle. I am getting a lot better than I was in the early days but the idea of going with the flow still brings me out in a cold sweat. I am a lot better but still will never be late often being annoyingly early. That said I am working on it. It is a developed personality trait from the injury. Is it worth getting upset about? NO. Sometimes on the road to recovery from anything there will be annoyances. These do not need to be a big deal and in time you can work on it. I am better but still some way off being chilled out. I have no doubt that I am a number of years away from arranging to meet my brother at 13.00 and not arriving at 12.15. Neil has spoken to me in the nicest possible way about this and I am improving and although still often early not as bad as I once was. My long term goal for this issue is to try and get to a point where I can go to Town and we may meet at one Pub or maybe somewhere else and nobody really knows what time. I would like to be relaxed enough to just go with the flow. This is very minor but mentally if you make a big enough deal out of it some potential harm can happen as it becomes a big deal.

Conclusion

In conclusion, I would like to thank everybody who has helped me along the way. I have received advice and guidance on many different levels and from many different people. When I mentioned this text to a few people there was some eye-rolling and talk of self-indulgence mumbo jumbo. This rocked me for a short period I mean minutes and opened up the self-doubt and am I doing the right thing emotionally? I managed to bring myself around quite quickly which is a further sign I am learning to evaluate emotions better. My aim in writing this is to raise money for some organisations that have helped me along the way and mean a great deal to me. I intend to give away 95% of any profit made. I am under no illusion that this is easier said than done but if I raise £10 in profit and give 95% away I am a £9.50 closer to the £20K target for raising money. It has also allowed me to reflect on the years that have gone by. Process the changes and how better to deal with emotions and challenges and just process and in a way deal with what has happened.

The important thing I have found is throughout my recovery I always wanted to be a nice guy and speak with people on as many different levels as I could. This helped my recovery and also helped me make some personality adjustments as I picked up advice and different perspectives along the way. When you are recovering from any aliment mental or physical the goal is to be in a place to accept the help given to you. If you cannot see the bigger picture and do not have the desire to get better you will not. This is true in many different walks of life and can be applied to a number of scenarios. If you set yourself short term goals first with the aspiration to achieve a more significant long term goal you must be at the stage where you see the benefit and want to achieve it. This is not easy and at many times through my journey have I wanted to give up. One time in particular which we discussed earlier. Whatever the end goal is, there are going to be some hard times. You need to surround yourself with good people and be prepared to ask for help. Talking about things that are troubling you is not weakness but can be a prevention against things getting much worse. I am not going to stand here and say it is easy to be committed to something or pick yourself back up when it doesn't quite go your way because it is not. What I can say is I am a very normal bloke who is not tough and certainly not known for his bravery so if I can do it so can anybody. As I said I am far from perfect and I had so much help from a lot of people to allow me to recover both physically and maybe more importantly mentally so I can lead a relatively normal life. When you go through life you always find yourself wishing for more and things and scenarios that you believe are more exciting. When the smallest pleasures are removed you understand that a normal life lived within your means with realistic goals and aspirations is a happy life. The biggest strain in life is pressure and stress. I didn't react very well to this a number of years ago and I still need to work on it today. Be prepared to apologise as your mental health improves. When you look back you may have said some things in frustration at your own situation and not acted in a particularly great way. Be prepared after time to realise this and apologise. In the earlier days, I did not react well to some things at work and I apologise for some things that I said to people. They were not said in anger but frustration at my situation. You were not to know this and for any distress caused, I do apologise. That said avoid chasing the quick fix that makes you happy by putting yourself under emotional financial and any other stress that means you struggle to look at yourself in the mirror. You will never truly be happy until you allow yourself to be. Stop chasing it and let it work itself out naturally. The world is always changing and it is a very different place from when I was growing up. Things that were funny then cannot be judged on today's accepted behaviour. The world has changed. What should always remain is to be nice to people. Black, white, rich, poor, gay or straight. Judge people on their actions and how they are. If they're not an ass be nice and get along.

At this stage, I would like to thank my friends and my wonderful family. All those at Ripley FC - Gus and Neil in particular. My solicitor, Helen. The great staff at the schools I have worked in. The lovely Emma and hopefully sooner rather than later the new Mrs Munro. A special thanks to the NHS and everybody I had contact with in my recovery, Everybody at St George's Hospital with special mention to Dr Martin and the charity fundraising team that sorted out and supported me so well through the marathons. The great staff at St Peters Hospital and the Ted Bradley Unit (Bradley Walsh) who gave me the best chance and worked with me to achieve my maximum. I have come into contact with so many medical and legal contacts that need a mention so rather than miss anybody – THANK YOU ALL. Without exception the kindness support and at times full care has been incredible. 95% of any profits made for this book will go to organisations that have helped me and a mental health charity that is to be discussed. I believe at this time with the pandemic and the heartache around the country and world this is hugely important.

Don't waste your life commit to things all you young people focus and work hard. Not just young people anybody for that matter. Make sure you have fun I certainly did but do not do it at all costs. Work hard, set goals and commit to everything you wish to achieve. If you don't quite get there do not blame others or circumstance refocus your attention try again or set more realistic goals. If you need it ASK FOR HELP. No situation is ever as bad as you think it is in your head. ASK FOR HELP. Whatever you do in life, BE ALL YOU CAN BE.

A Message from The Author

The proceeds from this book will be distributed as follows.

NHS - 30%

St George's Hospital - 20%

CALM - 20% - www.thecalmzone.net - 0800 585858

Bradley Walsh Unit (Ted Bradley Unit) - 15%

Hinchleywood School - 5%

Grace Dear Foundation - 2.5%

Ripley FC - 2.5%

Iain Munro - 5%
towards my teacher training year – if and when I get to it!

Available worldwide from Amazon

www.mtp.agency

www.facebook.com/mtp.agency

@mtp_agency

Michael Terence
Publishing

Printed in Great Britain
by Amazon

58819947R00059